ONLY AN EXCUSE?

ONLY AN Excuse?

1993 AND 1994

PHILIP DIFFER

MAINSTREAM
PUBLISHING

EDINBURGH AND LONDON

First published in 1995 by
MAINSTREAM PUBLISHING COMPANY (EDINBURGH) LTD
7 Albany Street
Edinburgh EH1 3UG

ISBN 1 85158 699 7

A catalogue record for this book is available from the British Library

Typeset in Garamond

Printed and bound in Great Britain by Butler & Tanner Ltd, Frome

For Ann and Philip

CONTENTS

PRE-MATCH DISCUSSION

25 June 1995, 11.58 a.m. (just before *Little House on the Prairie*)

It was, undoubtedly, the toughest decision of our lives.

It had trod the boards of a hundred theatres, it had infiltrated the video recorders of a million households; now, finally, the bookshops of the world – or at least Scotland – would play host to the words that were *Only An Excuse?*. We were talking book (one of those things with words and pictures in it).

Was our great, wee footballing nation (we are great again, aren't we? I mean, as I write this, we've only got to stuff the Finns and ream a draw out of the San Marinoesians to qualify for England) . . . (aw naw, as you read this, are you saying, 'Could he no' have shut up?' Have I rummelled up the gods of fate again?) . . . Where was I? Oh, aye . . . Was our no' bad, all things considered, wee footballing nation ready for such a thing?

What were the implications of such a publication? What happens if it gets into the wrong hands? Some sort of Socceroke? An epidemic of impersonationitis? Punters hitting you verbatim with a mingin' McIlvanney or a dodgy Dougie Donnelly? 'Watch out, boys, he's gonnae pull a Chick Young on us . . . "Ho! Ho! Ho!" . . . too late.'

In the end, we thought, 'They've heard the tapes, they've seen the stage show, they've pirated the video, maybe they'd like to see the words, maybe even read them, maybe have a laugh.'

So, here it is, we published and we've been damned, but we still felt this neo-Freudian, post-Nietzschean analogous study of our own mortality through the metaphor of fitba' would benefit from, by way of an introduction, a few chosen words from a soccer celebrity or a media pundit or even Jim Farry, but they all said they weren't 'mentally attuned' for the job.

So, in the time-honoured *Only an Excuse?* tradition, we made some up and displayed our intentions with an all-out attacking formation led by four forewords.

The choice is yours.

Foreword by

ARCHIE MacPHERSON

'Wooaafff!!! There's a neat touch and . . . *glorious little goal for Rangers!!!*'

Yes, no doubt about it, this is what football is all about, goals. Goals by whatever team upon which your allegiances, however misguided, however stupid – they are *your* allegiances and I respect that – have been most loyally attached.

Of course, I should in fact point out that I, being a football commentator, am of no fixed allegiance and only used the Glorious Rangers as an example because they were the first team that came to mind, purely by chance.

To me myself, personally, it is nothing personal to me but you know, I put it to you that football has lost its way, it's lost, if you like, not to put too fine a point on it, its allure, its lustre, its *je ne sais crois*. The carnival atmosphere reminiscent of a medieval fayre on the village green has gone, let's be perfectly clear about that, and in its place we have a cynical, businesslike mentality that puts profit before punter, bonds before Bovril, progress before pie.

And as for the media? Wooaafff!!! You know, some of these youngsters playing at being broadcasters and journalists should stop trying to be people and concentrate on being personalities. Give the fans what they think they want, opinions, not necessarily your own, of course, you don't need to believe what you're talking about, you don't even need to *know* what you're talking about just so long as it sounds as if you do. Because, the ordinary punter, God bless him or, indeed, her, let's not be sexist, the sort of person like you who is reading my words here and now, as I speak, in the written word, doesn't have the outstanding mental dexterity of your average media pundit and needs, *demands*, that we do their thinking and opinionating for them.

Gentlemen of the media, it is a privilege to wear the mantle of responsibility we have towards these millions of people out there who, through no fault of their own, are not as enlightened, nay, brilliant, as us, so I say to you now, and let's be quite clear about this, surely, *surely*, it's time to stop patronising the plebs and cut out the verbosity that is dragging our game down to the depths of quality intellectualism.

As the late, great, big man himself, Jock Stein, once said to me: 'Archie, away and gie us peace.'

Foreword by

CRAIG BROWN

When I heard that I had been appointed manager of the national team the first thing I did was write to Dixon Blackstock to complain, most vociferously I may add, about my appointment. But once we had got a couple of good results – the 2–0 destruction of San Marino springs to mind – and lost by a dodgy penalty against the Russkies (great for getting the Scottish chip on the shoulder back in place), I started to think I wasn't such a bad appointment after all.

I'm not saying that, at times, things haven't been tough. Over the last few months there were times when I considered packing in football altogether and applying for the Hearts job but, thankfully, through my meditational trances – I watch a lot of Hibs – I achieved the inner strength to see me through to my nirvana.

State of mind is so important. Someone once recommended Yoga to me and although I admire the ex-Bairns captain, I still think he's too . . . how can I put it? Too Scottish to play for Scotland. Drugs, however, is a bad thing. I remember being at a Player of the Year occasion when I thought someone had slipped LSD into my Malibu and lemonade. Turned out I was simply suffering the effects of listening to John McCririck's after-dinner speech.

But the greatest tonic of them all is – no, not Buckfast –

laughter, and I'd like to think Scotland have given the fans more than enough to chuckle at over the years. I know that Ally McLeod has virtually cornered the market in hilarious Scotland mishaps but my old mate and guru, Andy Roxburgh, had his moments too – and I don't just mean the one you'll be reading about in this book. What about him and Richard Gough, arm in arm, waving to the fans? What a joke that was!

But, when all is said and done, there's no point in laughing if you're not winning or drawing or just getting gubbed by a jammy, fluky goal. True, it's good to be able to laugh at yourself but it's even better to laugh at someone else.

So, as we, without complacency, march to glory, tell proud Edward we're on our way and spare a thought for Wales who are now what we used to be. Wales have become the Scotland of Britain and there, but for the grace of God or a referee, go us.

Foreword by

DENIS LAW

Only an Excuse? . . . Only . . . an . . . Excuse . . . question mark.

Well, you know, as I say, for me, football really is the beautiful game, beautiful but crazy, crazy but not criminally insane, right? Let's keep Wimbledon out of this. But no, yes, you know, as I was saying before I rudely interrupted myself, football, it really is a crazy game, it is. Crazy, mad, aff its heid.

If Scottish football, right, if Scottish football was a dog, it would be a terrier, of course, but it would be put down for having distemper or rabies or something, because . . . because . . . when I was with Turino in Italy which, for me, is still the best place to play in Italian football, what I found was that I hated it, so I came back and that's about it but, hey, listen boy, have you been watching *Match of the '70s* on BBC 1? Now that was football. Did you see me? Like a mongoose I was, I had it all. The speed, the face, the hairstyle and, you know, people still come up to me and say, 'Denis, what about that time you back-heeled the ball for Manchester City into the net against Manchester United and thus doomed a great club, who had been more than good to you in the past, to the total humiliation of relegation?' and I say, 'The one where I back-heeled it in and thus doomed the great Manchester United, who had been good to me in the past, to the total humiliation of relegation and walked away from the goal traumatised for life? I never think about it' because, you know, as I say, don't look back, unless Billy Bremner's chasing you.

Now, let us play and let us look forward to the Eurovision Championships and let's just hope it all goes right for Scotland – England get gubbed – and we go out and stylishly and with a bit of a swagger, don't make an arse of ourselves because, let's be honest, the English media will be waiting to pounce. John Motson, the talking car-coat, Brian Moore, the thinking man's baldy git and, of course, not forgetting, as if I could, the hammer of the Scots, the man who can drink his Bovril and stir the thick stuff at the bottom of the cup at the same time, *him*, Be-*Hill*-zebub, *that, it,* Jimmy Hill. Can't you just see his coupon if we do badly? Can't you just smell that roasted cheesy grin or that self-satisfied smirk or, worst of all, the insincere, patronising frown?

So, you know, as I say, that's why I ask, I insist, I implore every Scottish football fan to watch, every week without fail, *Match of the Day* with Jimmy Hill because I'm sure that, sooner or later, Alan Hansen is going to gub him. And that is something none of us would want to miss.

Hey, Jimbo, come on, how come you gave them two points?

Foreword by

JIM WHITE

Thanks, Denis, what a character.

You know, it really is a humungous honour to be asked to say a few words about something I don't really know anything about – humour – and it's even harder when it's not on autocue but anyway, right, here goes . . .

Hi, Jim White here and welcome to *Only An Excuse? Extra Whine.*

You know, the first thing people ever ask me when I stop them in the street and tell them who I am is: why were there no *Scotsport* cameras at Easter Road last season? Well, I asked Gerry and he said it was because Hibs fans were peeing on top of the OB unit. Now if that's true then that really is not on, not to mention unnecessary – after all doesn't Gerry come up with enough pish by himself? Ha! Ha! Nice one Jim, just a wee bit of a joke there to break the ice and show that I'm just one of the lads after all. But what lads, I hear you ask. Lads or boys? Boys as in Bhoys or boys as in apprentice, or hello, hello we are the billy variety?

Well, believe it or not, neither. But even if I was a True-Blue, Send her Victorious, No surrender, Son of William or one of the other mob it should make no difference to how I am perceived by my fans, nor should it matter for you dull, ordinary punters either.

Football shouldn't be about bigotry but, thank God, it is. Can you imagine how boring it must be pretending to support Partick Thistle or Clyde, affiliating yourself to a team purely for the football? It's unnatural. Where would we be without the hatred of an Old Firm clash? And don't look for the New Firm to provide any Boynean overtones. Unless they start importing Tims, because they're nearly all Proddies up that way.

So, remember, next time you're stuck in your car behind an Orange Walk, these men marching about dressed as Field Marshal Goering are what won us our democratic freedom from the tyrannical yoke of Rome!

How was that lads, too whimsical? No? Just the right note? Okay, thanks, mate, speak to you later.

1993

Only an Excuse? 1993
starred
JONATHAN WATSON and TONY ROPER
and was first performed at the Adam Smith Theatre,
Kirkcaldy on 7 May 1993

1993

ACT ONE

(The atmosphere is building up. The buzz of anticipation, the murmur of expectation, the rustle of crisp pokes mingle freely together against the backdrop of some of Scottish football's most odious soccer anthems disguised in the musical style of Richard Clayderman. Suddenly the peace is shattered by the awesome power of a BBC sound effects disc thunderclap. The lights flicker, then plunge into darkness. You could hear a pin drop . . . if it wasn't for the voice booming out over the theatre's public-address system.)

WILLIAM McILVANNEY

. . . and on the sixth day God was bored out of his skull, so he spake unto what he had created thus far, saying, 'Where there be harmony let there be discord, where there be unity let there be divisions, where there be tolerance let there be suspicion, where there be Proddie let there be Tim, where there be bigotry let there be bampotry, where there be balloons let there be broadcasters, where there is truth let there be exclusives, where there are phoneys let there be phone-ins, where there be a nation let there be late injury call-offs, where there is sanity let there be football.

(The build-up continues. Cue the music. Grand, dramatically Scottish epic 2001: A Space Odyssey *meets* Take the High Road *music. We reach a crescendo, fever pitch. The curtain rises on a bleak terracing sparsely populated by some petrified, bunneted dummies. Into their midst step the players, uttering words of earth-shattering magnitude.)*

BOTH
Erra macaroon bars and the spearmint chewing-gum!
Erra macaroon bars and the spearmint chewing-gum!

TONY
Erra disgusting greasy pies . . .

JONNY
Erra cold bovrils . . .

TONY
Erra programmes . . .

JONNY
Erra cheezy meat rolls . . .

TONY
Erra souvenir spe-shee-ell!

(They look around hopefully, but there are no takers.)

JONNY

What are they like, eh? What are Scottish football fans like?

TONY

Exactly. You lay on all these facilities for them and they just don't appreciate it.

JONNY

Sometimes I wonder why I go to all this effort.

TONY

I'll tell you why you go to all this effort – because you love the game.

JONNY

What, even when I'm hating it?

TONY

Especially when you're hating it. That's the thing about Scottish football. You love to hate it but you also hate to love it. It's the ultimate addiction. And see once you're hooked, there's no cure.

JONNY

I know what you mean. It's that feeling you get, that no matter where you are in the world, at quarter to five on a Saturday, you've *got* to know the results.

TONY

Next thing you know, you're runnin' about like a mad skull lookin' for the Sports Edition of the *Torremolinos Times.*

JONNY

Or lyin' on a beach in Florida tryin' to get Radio Clyde on your trannie.

TONY

And then you've been on the phone for half an hour trying to get through to your pal back hame, and you finally manage and it's: 'Hey Tam, it's us . . . aye . . . listen . . . no, no, listen . . . we're having a brilliant time here, aye. How did the boys get on?'

JONNY

They got beat four–nothin'!

TONY

Right, thanks for ruinin' my holiday, ya bastard.

JONNY

But that's the great thing about football, isn't it? For every low there is, you know that just round the corner, there's an even lower one.

TONY

Ach, never mind. Always look on the bright side, eh?
Look at all the intellectually stimulating points
football's gave us, like . . . well . . . like . . . er . . .
there must be somethin' . . . Oh, I've got it!
Remember that time the *Daily Record* asked the
managers to pick their favourite pop stars? There were
a few shocks there, eh?

JONNY

Tommy McLean picked The Eagles . . .

TONY

Jim Jefferies picked Neil Diamond . . .

JONNY

Alec McDonald *didn't* pick the Larkhall Accordion
Band.

TONY

And look at all the classic confrontations that we've
seen.

JONNY

Oh aye: Celtic versus Inter Milan, Rangers versus
Moscow Dynamo, Aberdeen versus Real Madrid . . .

TONY

Gough versus Roxburgh, Souness versus Aggie, the tea-
woman at St Johnstone, the Celtic board versus the

rest of the world.

JONNY

And see when it comes to officials, the Scottish
Football Association is right up there with the Albanias
and Greenlands of the soccer world.

TONY

I'll tell you something else. See our referees? They're
never wrong, never make a mistake.

JONNY

Absolutely.

TONY

Oh, definitely.

JONNY

FIFA want to make them professionals now.

TONY

Well, they should. They should get paid the going rate
for the job because they deserve it – they're worth
every penny. Especially Big Les Mottram.

JONNY

Old Hawkeye himself.

TONY

Partick Thistle versus Dundee United. Paddy
Connolly, the United striker, gets the ball and he hits
it a cracker, scuds it right into the back of the Thistle
net. Hits the stanchion, bounces back out again. So
the Thistle defender, he picks the ball up, hands it to
his goalkeeper. Well, it's a goal, in't it? Well, at least a
penalty, eh? Nah. Big Les is mincing up the track
waving play on, play on.

Now, out on the trackside, Jim McLean's goin' off
his head. His face is like a psychopathic beetroot. His
specs have all steamed up, and his hair is going up and
down like a pedal-bin lid. He's got the corner flag like
a harpoon and he's after the linesman and you can
guess where he wants to shove it.

Now, meanwhile in the Thistle dug-out, John
Lambie is displaying solidarity with a fellow manager
by turning his head away . . . then pissing himself
laughing.

The Thistle fans, they're no' quite so diplomatic.
They're flicking the vickies at the Dundee United
crowd, who by this time are starting to turn ugly –
well, they were always ugly but you know what I
mean. Anyway, the United fans are threatening to
invade the pitch – all fifteen of them.

All hell's about to break loose. The riot squad are
gonnae arrive, so Paul Sturrock, he decides to hide the
United fans inside his coat. Meanwhile, Papa Doc
McLean is still remonstrating with Big Les before, in a
fit of pique, turning and challenging the entire
enclosure to a square go. Dozens are injured in the
rush to take him on and that's all because our referees
never make a mistake.

JONNY

I suppose the referee's just got to call it as he sees it –
only, that time, he didn't see anything; so what he saw,
he didn't actually see.

TONY

Well, can he no' just come out and say that!

JONNY

I suppose it's that veil of secrecy that surrounds referees
that makes us suspicious of them.

TONY

Veil? More like an apron, if you ask me. Remember the
Jim McCluskey of Stewarton affair? The ever-paranoid
Celtic fans were so suspicious they actually put a
private detective on the man – and there, was he no'
discovered at the scene of an Orange Walk.

JONNY

But was he actually *in* the walk?

TONY

No, he was too drunk to walk. He was doin' the
Orange Crawl along the pavement.

JONNY

You see, that's the one big blight on the game. Well, I
mean, apart from the bigotry, religion should never
come into football.

TONY

No, I couldn't agree with you more. Oh, wait a
minute, here are the teams comin' on.

*(They discard their wares temporarily and move
menacingly towards the edge of 'the pitch'. Venom oozes
from every pore.)*

TONY

We'll gie them a cheer on – Die! Die! *Die!* Ya Hun
Orange, Proddie dog, scum-of-the-earth Dobs! Daniel
O'Donnell, ya bas! *(Turns to Jonny.)* Nae offence.

JONNY *(accepting the apology)*

None taken. *(Turns his attention to the pitch.)* Away
back to the Vatican, ya Mickey, Tim, lovin'-every-
minute-of-the-royal-family's-agony bead-rattlers! *(Turns
to Tony.)* Nothin' personal.

TONY

No problem.

JONNY

Right, so much for our team, now for the opposition.
Who is it we're playing?

TONY

Eh . . . Raith Rovers.

JONNY

>Hey! Away back to Raith, ya Mickey, Hun, Tim, Proddie, lovin'-every-minute-of-Daniel-O'Donnell's-misery, ya bastards!

TONY

>Oh, hey . . . hey . . . hey, the referee *(he starts to sing)* . . .
>Who's the mason?
>Who's the mason?
>Who's the mason in the black?
>Who's the mason . . . *(Jonny's raised hand stops him mid-line as he reads from the programme.)*

JONNY

>The referee is Mr Brendan Communions from Coatbridge.

BOTH

>Who's the knight?
>Who's the knight?
>Who's the knight of St Columba in the black?
>Who's the knight of St Col-um-ba in the black?

TONY

>Oh look, a wee mascot.

JONNY *(he checks the programme again)*

>Five-year-old Paul Smith. What a big day for him, eh? A day that wee boy will never forget.

30

TONY

Aye. We'll make sure of that. *(He starts to shout at the mascot.)* Hey! Shortarse! Did ye no' know your jersey's no' supposed to hang out the bottom of your pants!

JONNY

By the way, the nurse is comin' to school tomorrow to check your head for bumps, and then she's gonnae give you a jag with a blunt needle and cover your fazog with purple ointment!

TONY

Hey, hey, and even although your teeth just need a wee polish, the dentist is gonnae give you gas – that's just to be rotten!

JONNY

And the next time you forget your kit, the gym teacher is gonnae make you play at British Bulldog in your vest and Ys!

TONY

That's so's the lassies will laugh at you!

JONNY

Your maw's a bun!

TONY

Your faither's a walliper!

JONNY

Your dug's a . . .

TONY

Hey, hey . . . he's greetin'.

JONNY

Well, I'm sorry; if he can't handle the big occasion he shouldn't be on the pitch. Go on away back to the nursery! *(Tony gets a bit emotional.)* What's the matter?

TONY

I'm sorry, I'm sorry, I'm sorry. It's just that, well, see every time I see an emotionally savaged wean being dragged off the park like that, I always get a bit emotional, you know, because for me, that's what Scottish football is all about.

JONNY *(not quite sure about this)*

How do you make that out?

TONY

Well, you see the psychological mauling we just gave that boy, right, that will cause him to grow up with a deeply disturbed, pathologically unbalanced mind. So, in our own humble way, we have laid the perfect mentality for a Scottish professional football player . . . or a mass murderer.

JONNY

And all this time I thought we just hurled abuse at them 'cause we were rotten bastards.

TONY

Oh aye, we're that as well, you know.

JONNY

Such a difficult decision for a boy to make all the same, eh. Maniac or footballer? I suppose he could combine the two and play for Airdrie.

TONY

Mind you, y'see, that is what makes Scotland so unique as a footballing nation. See, all the other countries, right, they can have all the ability, all the class, all the natural skill – but they don't breed the nutters like we do, the bampots or, as the press call them, the *personality* players. *That* is what Scottish football is all about.

JONNY

No, no, no. Being Scottish, *that's* what Scottish football is all about. Being paranoid, self-destructive, self-pitying . . .

TONY (*proudly*)
Aye, whau's like us, eh?

JONNY

I'll tell you who's fault it is that we're Scottish.

TONY

Whose?

JONNY

The English. They are what Scottish football is not all about.

TONY

How do you make that out?

JONNY

Well, without oversimplifying a highly complex issue, the reasons are threefold. One, they are English. Two, they come from England. And three, *that bastard Jimmy Hill.* They make us *feel* Scottish. Look, leaving aside the pointless paranoia and dwelling on the past, ask yourself this: see when it comes to the World Cup qualifying sections, how come they always get the easy teams? How come we get the hard teams? And how come they never got banned from Europe for the way they behaved after Culloden?

TONY

You're right, you're absolutely right. So being mental, paranoid, self-destructive, self-pitying and dwelling in the past, *that's* what Scottish football is all about, eh?

34

JONNY

Aye. Naw. Well, maybe. *(Confused.)* Look, let's hear what the Magnificent Monotone has to say about it.

TONY

Who?

JONNY

William McIlvanney.

WILLIAM McILVANNEY

When you're talking personality, you're talking person with a bit of nality. Someone whom the gods – or Ian Archer – have deemed special, a unique being with charisma and talent. Unless that personality is a *Scottish* personality. For in this footballing nation of ours the word 'personality' has come to be the recognised shorthand for one hundred per cent pure mental.

Then there is the question of nationality. Being Scottish is the only thing wrong with being a Scotsman. For to be Scottish is to be possessed by the demons of self-destruction. Scottishness being a towering triumph to the power of positive thinking – a *total* conviction in your lack of self-belief. A conviction crucial to the progressive stagnation of our game whose absence might have altered the course of our history. *With* self-belief, in 1885, it might have been Arbroath 36, Bon Accord 37. In 1967 it would have been Berwick Rangers 1, Glasgow Rangers 5. At Wembley in 1961 it could have been England 9, Scotland 4.

But as Scots we have no option but to treat victory and defeat the same because for every Bannockburn there is a Culloden, a Flodden, a Glencoe, a Hampden, a Wembley, a Costa Rica, a Peru, an Iran – and an Argentina.

('Ally's Tartan Army' music. Enter an ever-cheery Ally McLeod.)

ALLY McLEOD

Ach, tremendous, y'know, y'know, I mean absolutely delighted, y'know. I mean, when we went to the Argenteen we were a world-class side, y'know – I mean, that's world-class in a Scottish sense, y'know. Which is actually rubbish. But ach, well, I was delighted, y'know, 'cause I mean I was never worried, y'know. I knew that when the chips were down Scotland always rises like a Felix from the ashes, y'know. It's just that, well, after the Peru game, y'know, the chips weren't so much down as trampled into the lobby carpet, y'know.

WILLIAM McILVANNEY

William 'Bud' Johnston. The outlaw dopey wills. A one-off. A character. A true personality player. He'd had a cold. Normally he'd take some pils – about four cans – but on this occasion he sensibly opted for some banned tablets and his place in soccer's hall of shame was secured.

ALLY McLEOD

I couldn't believe it, y'know. See when I saw his urine sample, it looked just like a pint of lager, y'know. It was all we could dae to stop Wee Joe Harper from drinking it. But, ach, well, y'know what I mean, Wee Bud was no angel, y'know, but I mean he was no saint either. He was just your typical average Scottish bampot ball player whose loyalties were torn between the Scottish national team and the Scottish and Newcastle Breweries. I mean, just ask Denis Law.

DENIS LAW

Well, you know it's so true, you know, because on the international scene, right, well, you know *my* loyalties were torn, you know, they were torn between Scotland, right, the cunn'ry of my birth, England, the cunn'ry where I live, and Albania, the language that I speak, you know. Isn't that right, Ally?

ALLY McLEOD

Ach, tremendous, I was absolutely delighted, y'know. But Denis, I still maintain that we were never given the credit that we deserved, y'know. Well, okay, we were humiliated, ridiculed, gubbed. But we gave the nation the opportunity to wallow in self-pity and a brilliant excuse to get pissed.

DENIS LAW

But, you know, never mind the '70s, never mind the '70s, I mean, what about the '60s? We had some marvellous characters back then, you know, oh yeah, we did. That's when I had the reactions of a mongoose, not just the hairstyle. But you know, there was the Law Man, right, who was me, and there was the Law-Unto-Himself Man who was Jim Baxter.

JIM BAXTER

See nowadays, it's all about money. I mean, we weren't in it for the money, we were in it to compete with the Crerands, the Gemmells and the Johnstones – God, what bevvy sessions they were.

DENIS LAW

Wee Jimmy Jinky, wee Jimmy Jinky, boy, could he dribble. He couldn't row, but he could dribble.

JIM BAXTER

And Tommy Gemmell. Mind thon time he hit the bar . . . nearly broke his nose off the footrail. I'll tell ye now, see what I say nowadays to players like me is, dinnae be like me. Train. Train, train, train. Get yourself fit. Because that way, you can run between the pubs faster.

DENIS LAW

But, you know, when you're talkin' to someone who's shared a hotel room with Billy Bremner, right, and a hotel room mini-bar with Besty when he was at his worsty, you know, today's footballer is far too professional, is far too dedicated, is far too stupid to bevvy as much as we did and get away with it. Apart from say maybe Big Duncan Ferguson, right. Well, you

know, I bet you Jim McLean, right, the I.M. Jolly of
Scottish football, I bet you he had a few problems
there. Jim?

JIM McLEAN

Hello. You know, this whole Duncan Ferguson affair, it
really affected me. I was miserable, melancholic and
depressed and that's why I hated selling him. Because
he made me so happy. But honestly, the press and the
media have grossly exaggerated the antics of Big Mad
Dog Dunky.

DUNCAN FERGUSON

Aye, that's right, ken? See, I come frae Bannockburn,
like, and I'm affected by the history of the place, ken?
See how just before the battle, an English knight tried
to chib Rab the Bruce but Rab lamped him on the
napper with his axe. Well, I've always had a great
affinity with him. No' Rab the Bruce – the bloke that
got hit on the heid, like. Mind you, all that happened
a long time ago, in 1314, and that's about a quarter
past one, I think.

JIM McLEAN

Aw God. We done everything for that boy. Forty-year
contract, fifty pence a week pocket-money, steel toe-
capped trainers, club straitjacket and an executive
penthouse bedsit in Dundee.

DUNCAN FERGUSON

Aye, well, we've taken legal advice, like, and my agent

says we're gonnae take Jim McLean to the European Court of Human Rights because, in this day and age, no one should have the right to force *anyone* to live in Dundee.

JIM McLEAN

D'you see what I mean? I mean, people say I was too harsh on the boy but that's just rubbidge. Okay, I admit to, in the past, taking the odd maddie with Duncan but only when he did something to annoy me, like . . . being there. But, now, I feel I know the boy and I would never question his ability, I'd never underestimate his potential and I'd never stand behind him in a taxi queue. But that's all in the past, now that he's joined *them*. I suppose he'll be all right once Walter gives him the dos and the don'ts.

DUNCAN FERGUSON

The dos and don'ts? Brilliant, d'you hear that, Coisty? They keep pigeons at Ibrox!

JIM McLEAN

Ah well, his Dundee United career set the heather on fire, his Scotland career set the hotel furniture on fire, maybe moving to Glasgow will sort him out.

DUNCAN FERGUSON

Nah, I'll be fine, I'll just knuckle down and soon achieve the life-long ambition I've had for the last two years – to be top scorer at Victoria's nightclub.

40

JIM McLEAN

As it turned out he was fine. Obviously the code of
conduct at Ibrox is helping him mature – either that or
the court appearance put the shiters up him. But to be
honest, I think the media has got this all out of
disproportion. I mean, Duncan Ferguson's like Cliff
Richard compared to Chic Charnley. Mind you,
Hannibal Lecter's like Cliff Richard compared to Chic
Charnley.

*(Enter Chic Charnley wearing a mask like Hannibal
Lecter in* The Silence of the Lambs.*)*

CHIC CHARNLEY

So, they didn't want me. Never mind. Revenge is
savoury. Seen much of Gordon Smith lately? I have. I
ate him with chips. Washed it all down with a bottle of
Tizer. *(Smacks his lips.)* Now I fancy a nice plate of
home-made soup made from a nice bit of juicy Jimmy
Bone.

JIMMY BONE

I didnae ken whit ti dae with Chic Charnley. Things
got so desperate we even thought about givin' him
drugs to calm him down.

WILLIAM McILVANNEY

Valium?

JIMMY BONE
LSD.

WILLIAM McILVANNEY
Glasgow. Where life is taken almost as seriously as football itself. The tenth of July 1989. A date that will live in infamy. Glasgow Rangers parade their latest signing, Maurice Johnston, the club's first *known* wooden Catholic signing of modern times. The country was plunged into a cauldron of confusion, a cesspit of silliness, a chanty of chaos, as the fans, by the sash divided, united in their disbelief.

IRATE HUN FAN
What? Hold on a wee minute . . . Wait a minute. Are you telling me that Glasgow Rangers Football Club have signed Maurice Johnston? *That* Maurice Johnston? *The* Maurice Johnston? *It* Maurice Johnston? Right! Well, that is it! Scrubbed! That is me and Rangers finito! Right! The hat's goin' back, the scarf's goin' back. See that? The season ticket's away! And see that tattoo of King Billy on my arm . . . *(indicates his forearm)* . . . right, the arm's coming off.

No, no, no. It's nothing to do with bigotry or the fact that he is an ex-Celtic idolater. It's to do with meddling – meddling with the unmeddlible, right. It's to do with traditions, right, traditional traditions. I mean, I'm no bigot but . . . *No Surrender!*

WILLIAM McILVANNEY
But they had. While on the other side of the barricades

the subject being contemplated was high treason. A mere five weeks previously, the Celtic faithful had hail, hailed, the Peroxide Prodigal's return as the Second Coming, but now that the chants of *crucify him!* had died down, it was time for thoughtful reflection.

TIM FAN

Y'see, what you've got to understand when you talk about Maurice Johnston is that you're talkin' about something that hasn't fully evolved, something that's not quite human. Now, don't get me wrong, I've always said that Rangers should sign Catholics . . . but diddy ones, no' ones that can play. However, that's it, evil has triumphed, good has been vanquished, there we have conclusive proof – there is no God.

WILLIAM McILVANNEY

Thank you, Archbishop Winning. What made Johnston's about-face all the more surprising – or, indeed, galling – was his behaviour in a certain Skol Cup final. On being sent off against Rangers he committed the provocative act of blessing himself. His Celtic teammates were shocked – that he could still remember how to. In the ensuing rammy, Referee Syme was skelped on the melt by a fifty-pence coin and then there was an invasion of the pitch by the Celtic board who were looking for the fifty pence. Upon such moments was built the legend of MoJo which plumbed the heights of notoriety that day, the inglorious tenth of July, when Rangers paraded their stunned acquisition before a press conference.

FIRST PRESSMAN

Maurice, Maurice, how does it feel to have signed for Rangers?

MAURICE JOHNSTON

Well, I'm just delighted *(sniffs)* 'cause Rangers are the only club I've ever wanted to play for.

SECOND PRESSMAN

Graeme, Graeme, Mr Souness, your Majesty. How difficult a decision was it to sign Maurice Johnston?

GRAEME SOUNESS

Can I just say something here about Maurice Johnston. He's a better player than I first thought. He's quite simply a quality player who became available, and this club will always be interested in signing quality players – especially when it *really* stuffs Celtic.

SECOND PRESSMAN

Yeah, but isn't it also true that, perhaps because of his reputation, he wasn't wanted by any other club?

GRAEME SOUNESS

I don't know what reputation you're talking about. All I know is that he was wanted in Italy to play for Torino, he was wanted in France to play for Montpelier, he was wanted in Hollywood to play Bart Simpson.

THIRD PRESSMAN

Maurice, Maurice . . . to be honest, Maurice, in
many, many ways, aren't you just a lying wee shite?

MAURICE JOHNSTON

Oh, thanks very much *(sniffs)*. Do I not know you?

THIRD PRESSMAN

I'm Billy McNeill. I signed you for Celtic.

MAURICE JOHNSTON

No, no, I don't know you, no *(sniffs)*. You'd better
speak to my agent.

BILL McMURDO

May I be allowed to speak? I am King Bill McMurdo,
Agent Orange. I can confirm that after meetings with
the law lords that the law lords have confirmed that
the contract which Maurice signed was inadmissible as
evidence because 'Aye, awright, I'll dae it' written on
the back of a bookie's line isn't legally binding.

MAURICE JOHNSTON

Aye *(sniffs)*. I was really pleased with the ruling that I
wasn't breaking a contract, I was only breaking my
word *(sniffs)*.

WILLIAM McILVANNEY

In the end, Maurice Johnston's career at Ibrox was
relatively short, relatively successful, not exactly

incident-free and ended in a blaze of indifference when
he signed for Everton . . . reserves. With the promise
that he would never play football in Scotland again,
this time at least he kept his word. Because when he
came back, he signed for Hearts.

But let us not forget the legacy he left us, let us not
forget the man who didn't so much rise above bigotry
as crawl beneath it. Nor the contribution he made to
the ecumenical movement by being Scotland's first
Fenian Orange bastard. For those who know it, no
explanation is necessary. For those who don't, no
explanation will suffice. It's been written about and
sung about, glorified and vilified. It's historical and
hysterical, cynical and sinister, yet it's claimed our
game needs it.

It's two majestic dinosaurs locked in an epic battle
to win.

It's two drunk men wrestling in the gutter.

It's the Old Firm.

(Scotsport theme music.)

JIM WHITE

Hi, Jim White here, welcome to *Scotsport Extra Whine*.
John McCririck will be along later which means you
get your racing tips straight from the horse's arse. But
first tonight, on the eve of the big Old Firm match, we
can exclusively reveal that the First Panzer Division of
the Larkhall Accordion Band has surrounded
Coatbridge. The leader of Scotland's Catholics, Peter
Grant, has been unable to secure assistance from the
Vatican, so he's done the next best thing and called a

meeting of Monklands District Council. Reports of atrocities are flooding in. Gerry?

GERRY McNEE

Yes, that's absolutely right. I, in fact, can exclusively reveal that crack BB units are forcing captives to listen to bible-readings while hordes of ninja altarboys are off-loading guilt complexes on innocent passers-by. The village of Croy has declared itself a Hun-free zone and has launched a nuclear strike on Kilwinning. So, carnage, bloodshed and ethnic cleansing, that special Old Firm atmosphere, is building up nicely.

JIM WHITE

Certainly plenty of food for thought there to be regurgitated by Gordon McQueen.

GORDON McQUEEN

Oh, dref . . . derf . . . de . . . do . . . do . . . do . . . definitely. It's a game where the players give all they've got to give till there's no gave left to be guved and, of course, they've went and gone and gived some more gave. And that's their guv all gived, and of course the fa . . . fla . . . flo . . . flans . . . fans hate each other, so the atmosphere is quite spe . . . spa . . . spesh . . . spesh . . . horrible.

JIM WHITE

Gerry, would you agree with that?

GERRY McNEE

Well, rampant bigotry, religious intolerance, vile
suspicion and bitter, bitter hatred, yes, Scotland needs
a strong Old Firm. It's a matter that needs to be
addressed by a top reporter . . . but *Sportscene* prefer
to use Chick Young, the Elmer Fudd of Scottish
football.

CHICK YOUNG

Ho! Ho! Ho! Thank you, Gerry McNee, the voice of a
football. Yes, this is me, Chick Young, standing where
I am which is here, poised to interview men who know
the Old Firm upside-down and inside-out. Current
Ibrox imperial wizard, Walter Smith, his Majesty, the
Great Waldo, Prince of Orange, King of Kia-Ora,
Saviour of the Sash, Scourge of the Tims, supreme
architect of the Glasgow Rangers, the Gers, the Teddy
Bears, the Sons of Will-Yem. And Brady.

LIAM BRADY

Hi . . .

CHICK YOUNG

Liam, it's been a pretty traumatic time for you. I'm
sure you'd like nothing better than to just forget about
it and get on with your life.

LIAM BRADY

Yes, that's right.

CHICK YOUNG

Well, Liam, no chance. Ho! Ho! Ho! What a start to a managerial career. And yet, I remember so well that day in 1991 when the smoke blew out the chimney at Celtic Park and it was announced that you, Liam Brady, would be donning the managerial vestments. But since then, nothing, zilch, sod all, not a tosser, first Celtic manager to win heehaw and, consequently, some of my less charitable colleagues might say you are, therefore, in some eyes, a haddy, a tube, a diddy, a failure, a miserable failure, a clown, a dud, a reject, a balloon, a monkey, a disgrace to humanity. Liam, nice to see you.

LIAM BRADY

Yes, well, I'd just like to point out to them that the last four seasons haven't been entirely empty at Celtic Park. Since I arrived Ireland have won the Eurovision Song Contest twice.

CHICK YOUNG

Liam, without going on too much about Celtic, how come they're so rubbishy, pathetic, dismal, hopeless, absolutely duff, mince, pure pish – especially when compared with the mighty Rangers. As a Saint Mirren fan I'd be interested to know your thoughts.

LIAM BRADY

Yeah, well, I put that down to loss of form at crucial points of the season, namely the beginning, the middle and the end.

CHICK YOUNG

Off the park, too, things haven't been going too kindly for Celtic, but, without being too forthright in my misgivings, what a shambles! It's a disaster! You're skint, rooked, well and truly in the grubber! Cambuslang? Ho! Ho! Ho! Jackanory . . . Jackanory!

LIAM BRADY

Well, things might seem a bit uncertain at the moment but whatever happens the fans will notice one major improvement next season. Already the architects are planning an extensive ten-million-pound facelift on Tony Mowbray.

CHICK YOUNG

But what about that Celtic board – the Three Stooges meet the Four Horses Arses of the Apocalypse to form the Intransigent Seven. And what will the outcome be? Timageddon?

LIAM BRADY

Yeah, well, in referring to the board, they are trying very hard to raise cash, y'know. I mean, at Hallowe'en they organised a fundraising event.

CHICK YOUNG

And what was that?

LIAM BRADY

They all went out guising.

CHICK YOUNG

Of course you started the new season with your new backroom staff. Tell me, was it difficult convincing Big Joe Jordan to come off the broo and join Celtic?

LIAM BRADY

Ah no, Joe's a Celtic man through and through. He had no hesitation in joining the club – even though it did mean a drop in wages.

CHICK YOUNG

Well, he's back in the big money again. And, finally, Liam, without twisting the knife any more, would I be right in telling you that it was after the League Cup semi-final at Ibrox against the glorious Rangers, when once again it was a case of fail, fail, the Celts are here, that you finally decided to ex-communicate yourself?

LIAM BRADY

Yeah, well, after that game I think you're right, I did notice a significant change in the fans' attitude towards me.

CHICK YOUNG

The Celtic fans were saying that 'Brady must go'?

LIAM BRADY

No, the Rangers fans were saying 'Brady must stay'.

CHICK YOUNG

Well, Liam, good luck with your life in whatever you do now. If you'll excuse me, I'm away now to support Saint Mirren.

LIAM BRADY

Well, there he goes, Chick Young, the man with the best eyesight in Scotland. Well, you'd have to, to support Saint Mirren from the middle of the Copeland Road stand.

Ah well, things haven't gone right, ye know, they haven't gone right for me. But never mind, the old Irish saying pulled me through: one potato, two potato, three potato, four . . . if at first you don't succeed get out the bloody door.

Mind you, the thing about being with Celtic is that you're always compared to Rangers. But I have to say I've nothing but admiration for Walter Smith. What he's achieved in the last two seasons has got me mystified. Where does he get that spirit he instils in the team? Where does he get the talented young players? Where does he get those sleeveless cardigans?

Walter, good to see you, you're looking very smart.

WALTER SMITH

Aye, cheers, I always try to look particularly smart, you know. Seems I got a better deal with Ralph Slater than you got with Stuart Slater.

LIAM BRADY

Walter, listen, I meant to say, listen now, on behalf of

all the Celtic fans, thanks for losing 2–1 to FC Sofia. If it hadn't been for that result they'd still have to listen to Tiger Tim, you know.

WALTER SMITH

Ach, no bother. In fact, as that late winner sailed into the back of our net, I remember saying to Archie Knox, 'Ach well, never mind, at least we've cheered up the Celtic fans'.

LIAM BRADY

I have to say, though, Walter, that is some squad you've got over at Ibrox. Why, when I used to look in that Rangers dug-out it was frightening. That's probably because Davy Dodds was looking back at me, though.

WALTER SMITH

Ach, no, cheers Liam. Last season was particularly good, you know, for Rangers in particular, but obviously, I have to say, ultimately it was a disappointing and worrying year because, at this club, the priority will always be the stability of the House of Windsor. And talking of families with divine rights, how's the Celtic board?

LIAM BRADY

Absolutely great, brilliant. I mean, last season they organised the Jungle's last stand, you know, fancy dress, free captions competition, free ginger . . . that beats winning trophies any day, eh? Listen, how are the Ibrox board?

WALTER SMITH

Well, obviously, no problems – in fact, our board are particularly involved with the players. The chairman, David Murray, helps them with business matters; Donald Findlay QC advises them on legal affairs; and Ian Skelly has given Ian Ferguson tips on how to buy a second-hand car.

Well, Liam, if you'll excuse me, I'm away to ask Chick Young his advice on when to make my next move to sign Gordon Durie.

LIAM BRADY

Oh, sorry, I meant to say hard lines in getting knocked out the European Cup again, you know. But hey, listen, the next time you're over at Celtic Park, I'm sure if you ask, they'll give you a wee hold of theirs.

WILLIAM McILVANNEY

But, believe it or believe it not, there is just a bit more to Scottish football than sectarianism. Occasionally commercialism gets in the way . . . or does it? Maybe these two -isms are simply opposite faces of the same double-sided coin, living off each other in a mutually exploitative parasitical pact which bleeds the fans dry of their tolerance and their cash. For there is no shortage of inducements for the punter with a few pounds he can't really afford to spare. There is the ever-blossoming video market with a wide variety of similar tapes to choose from. There are videos about teams like the Saint Mirren story, *The Darling Buddies of Dismay*, and there are videos about players like the fly-on-the-kebab-shop-wall documentary on Ian

Durrant: *In Bed With Ma Donner.* And for the
intellectual fanatic – wherever he might be – there are
books, as reviewed by Radio Clyde supremo, Alex
Dickson.

ALEX DICKSON

Hello, Alex Dickson here. Now, if you, like me, enjoy
a racy read, a thought-provoking publication, a – how
can I put it? – an intellectually stimulating story, then
the book for you is *Selected Nursery Rhymes* by Jock
Wallace.

JOCK WALLACE

Er . . . Jack and Jill went up the hill to fetch a pail of
water; Jack fell down and broke his crown because he
wasn't fit, he had no character and the boy didn't
believe in himself.

ALEX DICKSON

I think you'll enjoy it. However, if you're more inclined
to, well, let's say the classics, if you're the sort of person
who likes your books with words in them, then the
masterpiece for you is the stunningly, imaginatively
titled *My Story* by Ally McCoist. The critics have
raved:

ANNOUNCER ONE

'Not bad' – *The Times.*

ANNOUNCER TWO
'Quite good' – *The Observer*.

ANNOUNCER ONE
'Average' – *The Guardian*.

ANNOUNCER TWO
'Jings Crivvens, what a book' – the *Sunday Post*.

ANNOUNCER ONE
'Superb. Better than Tolstoy, Dostoyevsky or any other bloke who writes' – the *Rangers News*.

ANNOUNCER TWO
'Satanic rantings of the Antichrist' – the *Celtic View*.

GRAEME SOUNESS
Can I just say something here about Ally McCoist. He's a better author than I first thought. Yeah, for sure, we had our disagreements in the past but I bear him no grudges or no hard feelings as I explain in *my* new book, *That Bastard McCoist*.

JIM McLEAN
Well, personally, I don't like the idea of players writing books because they only fill other players' heads full of ideas – well, the ones that can read, that is.

DENIS LAW

> Yes, but come on now, Jimbo, come on. We have to accept, right, that today's professional footballer, you know, he can secure his future by investing in, you know, in investments, right, which suit his personality, right. Now you've got Charlie Nicholas, you've got Charlie Nicholas of Celtic, right, he's invested in the social scene and bought himself a pub. Ally McCoist, Super Ally of Rangers, he's invested in his hobby, bought himself a racehorse. And what about Wee Joe Miller? Wee Joe, he's invested in property, bought himself a bouncy castle. Isn't that right, Jophes?

JOE MILLER

> No, it isnae right. You stop tormenting me. I am a mature man now and if you don't believe me I'll shoot you with my Martian death ray-gun . . . and then I'll tell my Uncle Bill.

BILL McMURDO

> May I be allowed to speak again? Yes, it's me, Uncle Bill McMurdo, the Prince of Dampness, sole representative of Mr Wee Joe Miller. I can confirm that Jophes is all growed up now because for the last two months he's been going to bed with the light *off*. Can I also just say that it's my job to ensure my clients make as much money as possible – to blow on booze and birds and then to tour the country holding question-and-answer sessions with the fans. Isn't that right, George Best?

GEORGE BEST

Yeah, well, that's right. I'm going to talk about the decade 1966 to '76, so if anyone can remember what I did would they let me know?

WILLIAM McILVANNEY

So, as we run down the tunnel of life towards the field of hope only to fall on our jacksies in the puddle of destiny, rest easy in the knowledge we are not the first and by no means the last to know how this feels.

(The half-time whistle sounds.)

JONNY

Is that no' the most pathetic excuse for a fitba' match you've ever seen?

TONY

Hey, by the way, that was rubbish, crap, pure pish.

JONNY

Putrid, rancid garbage. What's the score anyway?

TONY

I don't know, I wasnae watching.

BOTH

Erra macaroon bars and the spearmint chewing-gum . . .

(The players head off into the wings. The curtain falls and the lights go up.)

HALF-TIME

END OF ACT ONE

HALF-TIME
ENTERTAINMENT

SPECIAL ANNOUNCEMENT

THE STEVEY TOCHER TESTIMONIAL COMMITTEE
proudly presents
YET ANOTHER STEVEY TOCHER
TESTIMONIAL DINNER
at the Holidality Inn, Glasgow

featuring an exclusive auction of rare football memorabilia conducted by a right big star* from the world of soccer and including items such as:

- Another Scotland jersey said to be the one Jim Baxter wore at Wembley in 1967
- a Fergus McCann matching bunnet and moustache
- Paul Sturrock's big coat
- David Narey
- a sleeve from one of Mark Hateley's jackets (donated by Duncan Ferguson)
- the rowing boat that featured in the infamous 'rowing boat' incident at Largs featuring Jimmy Johnstone and a rowing boat

Tickets: £100 each or £1,000 for a table of eight.
Black tie. No colours. No sneaking in a carry-out.

*Okay, so it's Chick Young

WHO IS STEVEY TOCHER?

Steven 'Stevey' Tocher was probably one of the most average players ever to come out of or stay in Scotland. An all-round dud, he was hopeless anywhere on the pitch but, through doggedness, determination and threats of physical violence, he had trials with Dumbarton, Albion Rovers and Greenock Sheriff Court before moving to Italy where he signed for Serie Z side, Clemenza.

The highlight of his career in Italy came in a cup clash with AC Milan when he went for a fifty-fifty ball with the legendary Franco Baresi. Two weeks later, when he recovered consciousness, Stevey had somewhat lost his appetite for Italian football.

He returned to Scotland where he attended more trials than Donald Findlay. After these trials he had two offers to consider: a season as a sheepdog up in Oban or a one-year contract with Albion Rovers. Stevey couldn't face the humiliation so he took the job as a sheepdog. His movements around sheep soon attracted the attention of Aberdeen scouts but the dream move collapsed despite the negotiations being handled by his agent, Hughie the shepherd.

Posing like a haddie in a kilt, giving teams marks out of ten in the papers, writing letters, phoning phone-ins, playing in charity matches, trying to get arrested for fighting in taxi queues, Stevey tried all the usual methods of enhancing his profile but it wasn't until he started drinking heavily and bleating about how life 'wiznae fair' that fellow heavy-drinking bleaters with influence decided that if anyone deserved a testimonial it wasn't Stevey but we'll give him one anyway.

But the final word, the final, metaphorical 'ten pence for cup of tea', came from the man himself when, as he eloquently put it: 'It's no' ma fault I am pish at football and it's no' ma fault that I am skint, so gie us money. Cheers.'

Stevey X X X

JUST WILLIAMS

Hello! Hello! Who Are the Billy Boys?

A paranoid Tim guide to the Hunnic infiltration of Scottish football by revealing the true nicknames of our top clubs.

Rangers: The Sons of William
Hearts: The Cousins of William
Airdrie: The In-laws of William
Dundee Utd: The Arabs of William
Falkirk: The Bairns of William
Alloa: The WASPS of William
Berwick Rangers: The Wee Sons of William
Arbroath: The Red Hand of Lichties
Clydebank: The Bankies of the River Boyne
Cowdenbeath: The True Blue Brazil
Dumbarton: The Sons (say no more)
East Fife: The Fifers (Fife/flute, I rest my case)
East Stirling: The Shire (Shire horse, King Billy had a horse)

JUNIOR ROUND-UP

Western Stagecoach Ayrshire Challenge Cup –
preliminary bouts

Auchinleck	2 falls	Beith	1 submission
Darvel	0	Cumnock	2 submissions
Largs	1 ko	Whitletts	0
Maybole	0	Lugar	disqualified
Kilwinning	1 ko	Dalry	retired injured
Kilbirnie	1 ko	SAS	0

Don't forget your bootbrush! Ian Ferguson reacts badly to the realisation that he's being marked by Chris Evans

Movie news: Parkhead pontiff Fergus McCann captures the mood of the club in a scene from the new Celtic video, *For it's a Grand Old Team to Pray For*

Amidst growing rumours of interference in team matters, Rangers supremo David Murray calls a press conference to dispel allegations that he couldn't pick his nose

Hot on the heels of their loyal burgers and blue-cheese-and-onion crisps comes the new Rangers Indian restaurant, The Sash Mahal. Here vice-chairman Donald Findlay samples just some of the dishes from a menu which includes lamb tikka masonic, chicken billyanni and poppadobs

Building on youth: Tommy Burns' policies start to take effect with the introduction of Celtic's latest commercial venture, Cabbage-Patch Tims

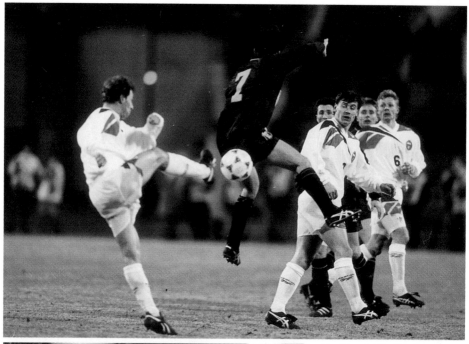

Pushing back the frontiers of medicine, Scotland striker Darren Jackson tries out a revolutionary new Russian treatment for piles

Prepare to meet thy dome. TV pundit Chick Young snatches a stiff drink before trying out a controversial new hair-restoring scalp rub

Great Scottish Football Traditions no. 21: Making an arse of yourself in a kilt

Behind the scenes at Radio Clyde: A porter takes another delivery of Derek Johnstone's custom-made Malteesers

1993

ACT TWO

(The interval is over. Bevvy has been swigged, Smartie supplies have been replenished, mortgages have been taken out against the cost of four Cornettos and a Mivvi. Football is about to be kicked once more. The lights go down, the curtain rises, music swells as the whistle blows, indicating the start of the second half. Two of the terracing dummies come alive and continue the story.)

TONY

Right, that's it started, we better get on. *(They get their newspapers out and study them avidly.)* Hey, I see Justin Fashanu's still with Hearts. I'd heard he was off to Italy to join AC/DC Milan.

JONNY

I must see that new video. Clint Eastwood as Maurice Johnston in *The Unforgiven*.

TONY

Hey, listen to this. Er . . . following his performance in the League Cup final, Keith Wright could be in line for a place on the Scotland bench. Craig Brown sees the big striker as the perfect sub, because he can dive! dive! dive!

JONNY

We're really lucky in this country, you know, having so many journalists. They know exactly what their readers want. No wonder they're known as fans with typewriters.

TONY

More like fannies with typewriters.

JONNY

But you learn so much from these experts. I mean, look at the *Whistler*, giving you all the very latest football gossip – four weeks after you've heard it in the pub. And I'll bet many's an argument has been solved by Bob Crampsey's 'Now You Know' in the *Evening Times*.

BOB CRAMPSEY

Yes, calling Big Numptie in the Cathkin Bar. In answer to your question, the Hi-Hi ended below the Bully Wee and above the Red Lichties only thirty-eight times that I can recall. However, in 1922, the Dry Boaks finished above all three but beneath the Soor Plooms and on equal points with the Mucky Shuchs. We'll get back to you on your other question, 'Where did Hibernian get the nickname Hibs?'

JONNY

And get a fascinating insight into the mind of the
modern-day footballer in *The Sun*'s 'Weekly Lifestyle'
feature.

TONY

Name?

JONNY

Steven Boghead Tocher. But my teammates have a
funny nickname for me – Stevey.

TONY

Team?

JONNY

Dumbarton Reserves.

TONY

D.O.B.?

JONNY

No, I'm a Catholic.

TONY

Married?

JONNY

No, but I've got hunners of burds.

TONY

Favourite TV show?

JONNY

Panorama or any other cookery programme.

TONY

Favourite comedian?

JONNY

Brian Martin of Motherwell.

TONY

Biggest thrill in football?

JONNY

Being on the bench for Dumbarton Reserves.

TONY

Biggest disappointment in football?

JONNY

Being on the bench for Dumbarton Reserves.

TONY

If you weren't a footballer, what would you be?

JONNY

On the bench for Dumbarton Reserves.

TONY

And if you still want answers, you can always watch
Sport in Question.

WILLIAM McILVANNEY

Or perhaps *Sport in* Stupid *Question* would be a more
appropriate title. The man who coined the phrase 'you
don't learn anything if you don't ask questions', had
obviously never seen this programme. For the answer
most people would like to know is: *where* do they get
the questions?

But what an education it is watching former
headmaster MacPherson prove himself a class apart
when it comes to schooling the audience in the art of
patronising both punter and pundit with equal
arrogance, and a technique the Doyen of Drivel
perfected on Radio Clyde's *Super Scoreboard*.

ARCHIE MacPHERSON

Well, what a cup tie this is. And it's Rangers sweeping
majestically forward as Stuart McCall pushes a long
bawl forward and it's amazing that even although
McCawll is smawll when he's got the bawl he looks
quite tawl and, oh, there's a neat touch from McCawll
and there's a glorious little goal for Rangers.

You know, as one looks around oneself at Ibrox
Stadium, this magnificent all-seater outdoor lodge, and
you see how omnipotent the team are, I put it to you,

Davy Provan, as an ex-Celtic man, does that get to you?

DAVY PROVAN

Well, Archie, hello Archie, to be perfectly honest, Archie, yes it does.

ARCHIE MacPHERSON

Good. So, with Rangers totally destroying Airdrie 1–0, let's go over to Love Street and Chick Young.

CHICK YOUNG

Ho! Ho! Ho! Yes, this is me Chick Young standing back where I was which is over there in the town of Mirren where my beloved Saint Buddies brilliantly gubbed some mob from the East Coast 2–0 with goals from new, young, teenage goalscoring sensation . . . er . . . Bobby Lavetry, who got one, and the other three scored by Cockles Wilson . . . er . . . Tommy Bryceland and . . . er . . . Eusebio.

But of course, the really important question is how are the 'Gers playing, Archie?

ARCHIE MacPHERSON

Oh, magnificent and majestic, well within themselves, this Rangers team have gusto, they have aplomb – ohhhh, they have just lost a goal. Offside surely!

DAVY PROVAN

Er, I'm afraid, Archie, you can't be offside from a

penalty kick. So Jimmy Boyle's goal stands and . . . I'm afraid we've got a bit of trouble on the touchline; the management team are out on the track, obviously furious about that penalty goal and, oh dear, Alex McDonald has just attacked Jimmy Boyle.

So, with the police now restoring calm to the Airdrie bench, let's take the roads and miles to Dundee and Dick Donnelly.

DICK DONNELLY

Yes, Dick Donnelly here at a rather dreich and drizzly Dens Park, Dundee, for this dramatic Dundonian derby between Dundee and Dundee United. Still no goals to report, no incidents, no corners, no shies – in fact, no teams, because the match, I've just been told, is being played at Tannadice.

DAVY PROVAN

So you'll have no idea what the teams are, Dick?

DICK DONNELLY

Well, actually, Davy, surprisingly I do. The teams in this Dundee versus Dundee United clash are . . . Dundee and Dundee United. And I can tell you, Davy, the latest score is nothing each in a dour, dull, defensive game, played in atrocious conditions with no skill or craft on display. A terrible advert for football but still not as terrible as Chick Young and Derek Johnstone's current car advert.

CHICK YOUNG
> Ho! Ho! Ho! Let's have a wee lookie . . .

DEREK JOHNSTONE
> . . . At all the cars made by Suzuki.

DAVY PROVAN
> Welcome back to *Super Scoreboard*. Now over to Castle Greyskull where Derek Johnstone is with Walter Smith.

DEREK JOHNSTONE
> Walter, that late equaliser, you must be gutted.

WALTER SMITH
> Well, obviously, I'm particularly disappointed. But you can't take anything away from Airdrie . . . apart from, well, you know, their chibs and Doc Martens.

DEREK JOHNSTONE
> Recently, Walter, you had your appendix out. Was it dead sore?

WALTER SMITH
> Not particularly, no.

DEREK JOHNSTONE
> Gonnae show's your scar then?

WALTER SMITH

Well, you know, obviously, there's nothin' really to see.

DEREK JOHNSTONE

Okay, Walter, that's what it's all about. And finally, Walter, I have to ask, for the fans will want to know – what happened to your appendix?

WALTER SMITH

Well, obviously, it was just a piece of raw meat that caused pain, you know, so Alex McDonald has just signed it for Airdrie.

DEREK JOHNSTONE

Thanks, Walter, different class. Now over to our Celtic correspondent, Hugh Keevins, who's with Paul McStay, one of that rare breed of Celtic players – one who *isn't* serving out a driving ban.

HUGH KEEVINS

It's been a difficult season for everyone concerned at the club but I put it you, Captain Paul McStay, that if Celtic had played as they can when they didn't, and hadn't played as they did when they didn't want to, then they wouldn't not be challenging as they could, if they were, which they aren't – it's as simple as that.

PAUL McSTAY

Well . . . there's a buzz about the place, the boys are

73

confident and hopefully we'll win something soon for the fans.

HUGH KEEVINS

The arrival of Lou Macari came as something of a sensation amid some scepticism but would it be fair to say that it was Lou's positive spirit which resulted in a spirited positiveness spiritually positivating the spirit of the team? Or was it more complicated than that?

PAUL McSTAY

There's a buzz about the place, the boys are confident and hopefully we'll win something soon for the fans.

HUGH KEEVINS

Thanks, Paul. Now it's back to the studio where I believe our first phone-in phone-caller is out there phoning in. So, caller, out phoning in the phone-in out there, you're through and what is the point you'd like to make?

CALLER ONE

Hello, panel? Right . . . hello, panel!?!? I'd like to speak to Chick.

CHICK YOUNG

Hello, caller, you're through.

CALLER ONE

Aye right, Chick, it's about this great Rangers team

youse keep goin' on about, you know. Can I just say I think Rangers *will* equal nine in a row. In fact, I think they'll win the League from now till doomsday and I blame Alan Davidson and the rest of the bluenose press, the referees, the linesmen, the SFA, the Scottish League, the media, the police and every other team in Scotland – except the Cel'ic – because they all lie down to Rangers, the sons of William; Hearts, the cousins of William; Airdrie, the in-laws of William; Aberdeen, the sheepshaggers of William. Every single one of them, they all lie down to them and know how? 'Cause they're all *masons!*

CHICK YOUNG

Can I ask you, caller, are you, by any chance, a Celtic fan?

CALLER ONE

Yes, I am.

CHICK YOUNG

Well, get it *right* up you! Next caller, please. Hello?

CALLER TWO

Hello! We are the Billy Boys! Hello, Chick! How's it goin', brother? Listen, Chick, see this 'we need a strong Celtic' rubbish. Where does that come from? Who needs a strong Celtic? I don't. I hate them. I *loathe* them. I *despise* them.

CHICK YOUNG

Can I ask you, caller, are you in fact a Rangers fan?

CALLER TWO

Yes, I am.

CHICK YOUNG

Well, carry on.

CALLER TWO

Aye, right, well, what I wanted to know is, see that crap, Irish skinhead singer burd, her that ripped up the photo of the Pope on TV? What's her name?

DAVY PROVAN

Hello caller, yes caller, well caller, Davy Provan here again, caller. Her name's Sinead O'Connor but that's not a sporting question.

CALLER TWO

Aye, it is. We want to name our Rangers supporters club after her.

DAVY PROVAN

Yes, it's an interesting new idea naming your supporters club after a figure you particularly admire, as they've done with the John F. Kennedy Celtic supporters club in Carfin and the Lee Harvey Oswald Rangers supporters club in Broxburn.

Next caller, you're through to the open line. What's

your question?

CALLER THREE *(irate)*
Hello, I'd like to speak to Hugh Keevins, please.

HUGH KEEVINS
You are to him in fact now speaking unto.

CALLER THREE
See, you're at it again.

HUGH KEEVINS
I'm at *what* again?

CALLER THREE
You think you're great, Mr Journalist, Mr Words Man.

HUGH KEEVINS
Can I answer the question now, please?

CALLER THREE
I haven't asked you one yet.

HUGH KEEVINS
No, perhaps not in as many words; but, in my
opinion, and I stress it is only an opinion, you are
about to ask me an incredibly stupid question; so,
what I'm saying is, I'll save you asking it by telling
you, right now, you're talking absolute rubbish. Does

that answer the question you haven't asked yet?

CALLER THREE *(happy and satisfied)*
Yes, that's fine. Thank you very much, ta.

JONNY
Hello, can I speak to the panel, please?

TONY
Oh, you're too late, it's finished now, wee man.

JONNY
Hello? Hello, operator? *Please*, I *must* speak to the phone-in.

TONY
No, listen, I told you. You're too late, it's finished.

JONNY
Just one more, just *one* more daft question, then I'll chuck it for good. Hello?! Hello panel, *please* somebody, anybody, *please* answer me, I'll even speak to Archie MacPherson . . .

TONY *(immediately rushing to his companion's aid)*
Put that phone down! You must be delirious talking like that, you know. *(Leads a shattered, shambling Jonny away and sits him down at the bottom of the terracing.)*

JONNY

I'm all right . . . I'm all right . . .

TONY

Are you sure? You want a cup of tea? A wee drink of Bovril? A swig of Benylin?

JONNY

No, I'm fine. I'm all right. I just overdosed on the dopes. This is the Radio Clyde equivalent of cold turkey – cold donkey.

TONY

Aye, I know what you mean. It's the same as that hollow pain you get deep in your gut when you know the World Cup finals are coming up and Scotland *are* gonnae be in them.

JONNY

Aye, well, no fears of that happening this time.

TONY

Aye, mind you, we better not get too confident wi' our complacency. I mean, knowing Scotland, a week after we've blown all our World Cup spending money, they'll discover the Italian players had too much testosterone in their blood or that the Swiss had too much Toblerone in their blood. They'll get chucked out and we'll qualify by default.

79

JONNY

Well, I hope not. We have our pride, you know. If we can't go to be gubbed in the finals as section winners or runners-up, then you can forget it.

TONY

Mind you, they're in America this year. It would be good to go there, wouldn't it?

JONNY

Oh aye. An' no' just for the fitba'; you could visit all the great battlefields, like Gettysburg, The Alamo, Los Angeles.

TONY

Oh, and that big fantasy park, what's that called again . . . oh aye, Cambuslang-World.

JONNY

Tom Cruise is a right Rangers man, you know.

TONY

Is he?

JONNY

Oh aye. Sure he was in that film, *Born on the Twelfth of July*.

TONY

Aye, right enough. Mind you, it's all very well, but what's the actual football gonnae be like, you know?

JONNY

I know. Sometimes you just can't help wondering where the game is going.

TONY

Aye. And we're not the only ones. Just ask Denis Law.

DENIS LAW

Well, you know, I think it's an outrage and a diabolical liberty that the World Cup finals are being held in a cunn'ry like the American States of United, you know. I mean, come on, they don't even like our beautiful game. What is their national sport anyway? American football? Baseball? Arson? Looting? I mean, what do you think, Alan Hansen?

ALAN HANSEN

Well, it's not just the fact that they don't give a monkeys about football. There are other problems, too. I mean, look at Davy Hay, he went over to manage their top women's team, Tampax Bay Rowdies, but at the end of the day, he had to come back from America because he couldn't learn the language.

DENIS LAW

But come on, Alan, I mean, as I say, is language and

the ability to communicate really *that* important in
football? Because, er, I've managed without it.

ALAN HANSEN

You better believe it's important; just ask foreigners
like Pieter Huistra.

PIETER HUISTRA

Hi, Pieter Huistra here, the Dutch cap that does score;
for sure, language is important in football, especially in
Scotland where, among the players, some are Scottish,
some are English, some are Irish, but most are rubbish.
But, you know, there is a great poetry in football –
none of it written by Jim Leishman.

JIM LEISHMAN

Ya whoor, ya bugger sir, eh?
Wallace, Wallace, get ti France.
Away from all your troubles.
Sing a song for Europe all about Hearts,
Called we're forever blowing doubles.

Mickey Thomas for shagging was stabbed in the arse.
Now he has to wear a nappy.
But who's screwing who at Marseille FC?
Who's Bernard on Tapie?

But is *our* game really in a mess?
Don't ask me, ask Graeme Souness.

GRAEME SOUNESS

Can I just say something here about Scottish football. Personally, I still happen to think that Scottish football is the best football currently being played anywhere in Scotland but this forty-four-game league programme is a killer. We've got to reconstruct the leagues into a Premier League of two – Rangers and Rangers Reserves – and the rest can do what they want because, without taking anything away from the Falkirks, the Dunfermlines or the Arbroaths of this world, who gives a toss about them? Apart from, I suppose, Danny McGrain.

DANNY McGRAIN

Well, Graeme, I'm afraid I have to say your plans for league reconstruction are totally unworkable, it would just be a fiasco, a complete disaster – so submit them to the SFA and they'll probably adopt them. But if you don't believe me, ask Kenny Dalglish, because he puts it a lot more succinctly than me.

KENNY DALGLISH

Could be . . . could no' be . . . maybes aye . . . maybes no . . . maybes Alex Ferguson.

ALEX FERGUSON

I agree with Kenny . . . I think. Okay, it's easy to criticise but there's a lot to be positive about, too. Tactically, Scottish teams are much more aware now. Aberdeen have abandoned the flat back four and have now got a spare man at the back to mark Brian Irvine.

And what about last season – Rangers' European run? All down to traditional Scottish fighting qualities as demonstrated by McCall, McCoist and McKailechenko. So, generally, I think Scottish football's in good shape thanks to the divine wisdom of the SFA and its inspiring leader – the Godfarry.

JIM FARRY

What have I ever done that they should treat me so disrespectfully? Come to think of it, what have I ever done? How can you say there's anything wrong with the current league set-up? Look at all the excitement on the last day of the season at Rugby Park when it was finally decided who joins Raith Rovers . . . in being relegated from the Premier League next season. Football's a funny game. Just ask Jiminy Nicholl.

JIMINY NICHOLL

C'mere, there's more. C'mere. I see Partick Thistle have got a new code of conduct for the players. If the players misbehave, the manager goes in a huff with them. It's called the Silence of the Lambies. C'mere, there's more.
What about Ivan Golac, eh? He's really got his finger on the pulse at Dundee United, hasn't he? He thinks Christian Dailly is a religious newspaper. But even worse, he thinks Davy Bowman is a football player. C'mere, there's more.
Cowdenbeath, what about Cowdenbeath? What a team they are. Their nickname's the Blue Brazilians but they've had to change it to the Chippendales because there's so many pricks in the team. C'mere, there's

more. Cowdenbeath, it's a great wee place. It's a bit quiet, though. I passed through it once. They had a sheep tied to a pole . . . called it a leisure centre. There's no more, right, that's all.

WILLIAM McILVANNEY
But if the press and radio is the bread and butter of our game then television is the Walls Viennetta where puddings get their just desserts from an ever-expanding menu of not just traditional fare but now Italian dishes too.

BOTH *(music sting)*
Goal – lato!

PETER BRACKLEY
And welcome back to *Gazzetta Football Italia*. And providing the expert analysis this week is Ray Wilkins. Hello, Ray.

RAY WILKINS
Hello, Peter. Good afternoon, ladies and gentlemen. Some fascinating matches in prospect this weekend. The sell-out derby matches between Sampdoria and Genoa, Inter Milan versus AC Milan and, of course, the big one, Paul Gascoigne versus bottom-of-the-league Reggiana.

PETER BRACKLEY
I was just wondering, Ray, did you happen to see the

Italy–Scotland match a few weeks back? Oh dear, oh dear, oh dear. Oh, what a catalogue of disasters, eh?

RAY WILKINS

A catalogue indeed. Brian Gunn went down for that first one in instalments. Then a defence-splitting pass by Baggio – who, incidentally, is nicknamed Steve Fulton by the Juventus fans – set up the second.

PETER BRACKLEY

Yes. Then, of course, the Jocks pulled one back with a Kevin Gallagher thunderbolt . . . off his shin, before the Italians hit them with a third. You know the Jockos, Ray, I mean, how were they that night?

RAY WILKINS

Over the moon.

PETER BRACKLEY

But why? I mean, their team had just gone out of the World Cup.

RAY WILKINS

Yes, Peter, but, more importantly, so had England.

PETER BRACKLEY

Yes, well, of course they don't like us, do they, Ray?

RAY WILKINS

No, they hate our guts, Peter. But there's a big support for Holland in Scotland and, you know, they've got a huge fan club for one of the old Dutch masters.

PETER BRACKLEY

Yes? Johan Cruyff? Ruud Gullit?

RAY WILKINS

No, William the Third.

PETER BRACKLEY

Well, before we stop talking about the Hairy Haggis brigade, Ray, did you rate Andy Roxburgh?

RAY WILKINS

Well, I don't know, Peter. Okay, so he's failed to qualify for the World Cup, but don't forget his European record. First Scottish manager ever to be caught shagging.

PETER BRACKLEY

A latest score just in: it's Udinese nil, Brescia one. A goal by Paulo Handsometti. And that's interesting, Ray, because am I not right in assuming that Paulo is Italian for Paul, which is actually Gazza's first name.

RAY WILKINS

Yes, ladies and gentlemen, you are indeed right in that assumption, Peter. But what is really fascinating about

Paulo Handsometti is that his second name *isn't* Italian for Gascoigne, although I will admit they are very similar.

PETER BRACKLEY

That's absolutely right and I have to admit I'd never noticed that before, but then, of course, I haven't played football at the highest level like you, Ray. And a score update: Udinese six, Brescia four.

RAY WILKINS

Well, well, well, ladies and gentlemen, would you adam and eve it, nine goals in thirty seconds. I think, ladies and gentlemen, mums and dads, boys and girls, that just might be some sort of record.

PETER BRACKLEY

I hate to contradict you, Ray, but recently, at a press conference, Gazza did nine *farts* in thirty seconds – but, well, maybe that's not quite the same thing. Well, we've all been marvelling at *Football Italia* over the past few months but what do the Italians think of our football, especially the variety played in the northern English shire of Scotland? We spoke to Atalanta's talented midfield assassin, Claudio Psychopathico.

CLAUDIO

Eh . . . como esta lasagne, asti spumante mario lanza paso la parmigiana ragu, ragu, ragu, mondeo imo spartacus, imo spartacus.

TRANSLATOR

Sure. Yes, of course. In Italy we all watch Scottish football on television where it is our country's top comedy show.

CLAUDIO

Si . . . si . . . Il buono, il brutto, il cattivo, mantovani di napoli esta gino ginelli tutti frutti cornetto cappuccino o sole mio tagliatelle carbonara.

TRANSLATOR

I think perhaps, however, there is maybe too much kicking in the Scottish game. In Italia, it is Serie A; in Scotland, it is more like Serie AAAAHHHH!

CLAUDIO

Travolta. Eh . . . Cortina ghia alfa romeo, alfa conn, fiato dolomite strada michelangelo garibaldi, la dolce ryvita, pirelli pizza mozzarella.

TRANSLATOR

He says there are players he admires. Walter Kidd, Neal Cooper and Shitey, Shitey, Shitey, Shitey Galloway. He's sure they would do well in Italy . . . if they ever started professional wrestling.

WILLIAM McILVANNEY

And after this high goal-esterol feast, what better to finish it off than the TV equivalent of a mug of Horlicks – *Sportscene.*

(Sportscene music theme-a-like.)

ROB McLEAN

Coming up on tonight's *Sportscene* . . . Our *usual* interview with Ally McCoist. A token reference to Celtic. Our obligatory *in-depth* interview with Ally McCoist. A dull piece about a provincial team and our *exclusive* interview with Ally McCoist. Hazel . . .

HAZEL IRVINE

Chick. What's the latest?

CHICK YOUNG

Yes, Hazel, and the latest news from the front line, hot off the press, hold the front page and the back page as well is . . . ask me after *Scotsport Extra Time.* But earlier this week I spoke to Rangers and Scotland striker, who else but none other than the grandmaster of disaster himself, Ally Alistair Coisty McCoist. First of all, Ally, are you missing the stookie?

ALLY McCOIST

Not at all, Chick, you can talk to me any time.

CHICK YOUNG

Ho! Ho! Ho! A stormer. But seriously, Ally, I would like to ask you how you like to get away from it all at your luxury villa at 28 Station Road in the picturesque village of Balmuir which is on the A68 just south of Eaglesham.

ALLY McCOIST

Well, that's right, Chick. When this house came on the market I moved for it quicker than a referee restarting an Old Firm game after Celtic have scored.

CHICK YOUNG

Ho! Ho! Ho! Nice one, Coisty. It really is a beautiful des res and obviously you've got very trusting neighbours because I notice you don't have an alarm installed. But moving on, Ally, you have achieved everything that a Scottish footballer can hope for – Skol Cup, Scottish Cup, League Championship medals, Player of the Year awards, double-glazing endorsement contracts – you must be loaded.

ALLY McCOIST

Well, Chicko, football is a comparatively short profession. Before you know where you are, you're too old and it's time to hang up your boots – or sign for Kilmarnock.

CHICK YOUNG

Ho! Ho! Ho! Another brammer! This is in fact your testimonial year when you will be rewarded for your services to the Sons of William. I have to ask you, Ally, don't you think there are others more deserving of such a testimonial for services to the club like, for example, off the top of my head – *me?*

ALLY McCOIST

Well, I don't know about that, Charley. These sorts of

decisions are made at the very highest level.

CHICK YOUNG

You mean, Her Majesty?

ALLY McCOIST

No, Andy Cameron.

CHICK YOUNG

Ho! Ho! Ho! A stonker! But Ally, let's get back to the night when the Euro dream ended. There were tears that night. Tell me, why were you greetin' like a big wean on the television?

ALLY McCOIST

Well, to be honest, Charley, I could give you forty-five thousand reasons.

CHICK YOUNG

Of course, those todally fantastic, quite unbelievable fans.

ALLY McCOIST

No, forty-five thousand was our win bonus.

CHICK YOUNG

Ho! Ho! Ho! A belter! And finally, Alzo, do you think monetarism combined with neo-Keynesian theory precipitates growth or is fiscal policy allied to liberal socialism the way ahead for the former USSR?

ALLY McCOIST

Well, that's right, Chick, this is something Ian Durrant and I were discussing just the other day and we both feel that market forces . . .

WILLIAM McILVANNEY

But we'll never know what the McCoist–Durrant solution to Russia's problems are because by now everyone has switched over to *Scotsport Extra Whine.*

TV VOICE

Scotsport. Another programme promoting health and fitness sponsored by *bevvy!*

JIM WHITE

And on tonight's extra whine . . . A more-exclusive-than-*Sportscene*'s interview with Ally McCoist . . . We'll be putting on our concerned faces and getting stuck into Celtic . . . And in our fantastic free-to-enter competition the chance to win a full set of irons . . . that's Davy Irons and his entire family. More details later, but first: what's the latest news, Gerry?

GERRY McNEE

Well, first of all, I can exclusively reveal that Ally McCoist will *not* in fact be appearing on tonight's programme. He's just received word that his house has been broken into.

JIM WHITE

Oh dear. What else, Gerry?

GERRY McNEE

England's Chris Woods looks set to regain his international goalkeeping spot. Manager Graham Taylor feels that Arsenal keeper David Seaman lacks spunk. Now normally we wouldn't give a monkeys about England but because it concerns an ex-Rangers player, we put it in.

JIM WHITE

Mmm. Interesting. Anything else, Gerry?

GERRY McNEE

Well, Scottish Television and Radio Clyde have responded angrily to Michael Kelly's accusation of pro-Rangers bias. In a joint statement issued today, both companies blamed the match blackout on Sporting Lisbon's financial demands, saying that there could be no surrender to such extortion. They also said they now deeply regretted not covering the match – especially as Celtic got gubbed.

And still with the Celtic Boardroom Saga . . . Things took another twist today when the rebels asked Sean Connery to join them. They see the former 007 as the ideal man to take on Michael Kelly, or as Fergus McCann calls him, Dr No. As I've said before, watch this space.

JIM WHITE

Thanks, Gerry, speak to you later.

Right, well, seeing as he was here recently with Germany and our intensive *Extra Whine* investigation has revealed he is a Protestant, that must mean Lothar Mattheus is joining Rangers. Earlier today I spoke to the Bayern Munich midfield *obersturmbahnführer* at his home in the beautiful German village of Bayern on the Spanish border.

Lothar, *bonjour, ich bin ein binliner*. Voulez-vouz wantez to flit to Scotlando and jeux sans frontières for der teddy berren?

LOTHAR MATTHEUS

Well, you know, for sure, as a professional footballer, I am always look for exciting new challenge like playing fifty games a season in ze pissing rain, posing like a haddie on ze fashion pages of ze *Daily Record* and, of course, the ultimate challenge – winning Star Check in the *Sunday Mail*.

JIM WHITE

Lothar, *merci beaucoup* very much, all the best to you, the burd and the wean.

Well, Gerry, what do you think about that?

GERRY McNEE

Interesting.

JIM WHITE

Isn't it.

GERRY McNEE
  Yes.

JIM WHITE
  Right, Gerry, thanks. Well, at the start of the season
  Europe beckoned. Two rounds later, Europe was
  waving ta-ta to Scotland's representatives. Personally, I
  happen to think Rangers should have been seeded.

GERRY McNEE
  They were.

JIM WHITE
  In order to get an easy team.

GERRY McNEE
  They did.

JIM WHITE
  After last season's magnificent European run which is
  worth slabbering over again . . . The first game,
  Marseille at Ibrox. Rangers, ravaged by injury and, of
  course, the *three* foreigners rule.

GERRY McNEE
  Well, that's absolutely right, Jim. But on the night
  Rangers, it seemed, had *four* foreigners present
  Hateley, Steven, Mikhailechenko and Houdini.

JIM WHITE

Ha ha! Very good, Gerry. Gordon, what were your recollections of that night?

GORDON McQUEEN

Well, me . . . persil . . . presely . . . personally, what intrigued me was the clash of styles – between Davy McPherson's bouffant and Rudi Völler's perm.

JIM WHITE

Yes, what impressed me that night, despite all that rain, was the remarkable staying power of Dave McPherson's styling mousse. Davie Cooper?

DAVIE COOPER

Rangers.

JIM WHITE

Thanks, Davie. On to the second game in Bochum, which is in Germany, to play the Russians; again Rangers *decimated* by injuries but, Gerry, they got the result.

GERRY McNEE

Yes, thanks to a spectacular strike by that hard-working professional Protestant, Ian Ferguson.

JIM WHITE

Hold on, Gerry, how do you know Fergie's a Proddie?

GERRY McNEE

Because he looks like one.

JIM WHITE

Right, Gordon. Spartak Dynamo CSKA Moscow or whatever they were called: pish, weren't they?

GORDON McQUEEN

Well, they were disprin . . . disappearing . . . no . . . no . . . disappointing, but I don't like to criticise fellow professionals so I'll just say they were utter crap.

JIM WHITE

Tough talking Gordon. Davie?

DAVIE COOPER

Rangers.

JIM WHITE

Then it was on to Bruges and, again, Rangers *utterly* devastated by injuries but, Gordon, they got the result.

GORDON McQUEEN

Well, yes, they did, after losing a . . . go . . . ga . . . go . . . goldfish . . . goal to the Belgians from Poland but they fought back with an equalizer from Pieter . . . Hoos . . . Pieter Hoos . . . the Dutchman.

JIM WHITE

And then, of course, came the return at Ibrox with
Rangers almost *wiped out* by injuries but, Gerry, they
got the result.

GERRY McNEE

Yes, the ball fell to the feet of Scott Nisbett and with
the fans all thinking 'Don't just do something, stand
there', he sent an unmeanable shot into the back of the
net. Now, once again, I thought, the crucial man for
Rangers on the night was the diddy in the opposition
goal.

JIM WHITE

And, of course, Davie Cooper, you predicted Moscow
were starting to come good as they lost 6–0 to the
Frogs.

DAVIE COOPER

Rangers.

JIM WHITE

Then, of course, came the Marseille ticket-allocation
scandal which meant only a mere thousand tickets for
the loyal legions of Luther. Gerry?

GERRY McNEE

Yes, well, a tragedy not just for football but for culture
in general because I'm sure more Frenchmen would
love to have heard five thousand Scotsmen singing

such traditional ditties as *Le Sash*, *Surrender Non* and *Bonjour, bonjour, nous sommes les garçons de Billy*.

JIM WHITE

And then came the match itself. Apart from the final score – another great result for Rangers – it was a tight match. Not a lot of exciting play and it has to be said, from the purists' point of view, a disappointing game . . . but sod the purists, it was another great result for Rangers. Gordon?

GORDON McQUEEN

Oh, great grame . . . game, great team Marseele, great players, Voller . . . Bostic . . . Patrick Swayze . . . Peely . . . Wally . . . Wee Alan Boli. Great strike by Durranty, great result, rubbish game but a great rubbish game for Rangers.

JIM WHITE

So it was all down to the last match and the task couldn't be clearer. Rangers had to beat the Russians and hope that Bruges could tame the tadpoles. But it wasn't to be, was it, Gerry.

GERRY McNEE

No, it wasn't, Jim. I'm afraid Rangers' luck finally ran out, or, put another way, they came up against something they hadn't encountered before in the competition – a goalkeeper.

JIM WHITE

    It wasn't a match for the faint-hearted was it, Gordon?
    What about Richard Gough. That was brutal.

GORDON McQUEEN

    Yes, all that blood on his face.

JIM WHITE

    Well, actually, I was referring to his haircut. So it was
    AC Milan versus Marseille in the final. Who did you
    fancy to win it, Davie?

DAVIE COOPER

    Motherwell.

JIM WHITE

    And, of course, without in any way passing any
    comment on the outcome of the UEFA investigation,
    the cheating French bastards won. A last word on the
    subject, Gerry?

GERRY McNEE

    Yes, well, when Rangers went out of the European
    Cup, it was a sad night not just for the club but for
    the whole of Scotland, who were right behind Rangers
    throughout this campaign.

JIM WHITE

    My arse.

WILLIAM McILVANNEY

Scottish football. Once a simple game played by semi-illiterates, now a multi-million-pound industry played by semi-illiterates. But is our beautiful game an empire upon which the *Sun* or the *Daily Record* never sets? Because if there is one word which sums it all up, it's – unpredictable. For all the world's a football stage and it's not us that play football, it's football that plays us in an ever-unfolding drama that arouses all the passion of Romeo and Juliet. We can be promised the glorious victory of Henry V then we can be stabbed in the back like Julius Caesar or stabbed in the jacksie like Mickey Thomas. And now the end is near and so we face the final whistle.

TONY

Come on, ya useless . . . are they no' the biggest bunch of diddies you've ever seen in your life?

JONNY

Oh come on, they're no' *that* good.

TONY

How long to go?

JONNY

We've played two minutes of injury time.

TONY

Ach, right, that's it, that's me finished. I'm done. I'm

never coming back.

JONNY

Me as well. Hey, there's your season ticket. *(Rips it up and throws the pieces into the air.)*

TONY

Hey . . . mine too, okay . . .

JONNY

Aye, away ti . . . *(Flicks the Vs.)*

TONY

Go'on get ti . . . *(Up-you gesture.)*

JONNY

Wait . . . Wait . . . haud on . . . Hit it! Hit it!

TONY

Cross it!

JONNY

Header it!

TONY

Blooter it!

BOTH

Gooooallll!

TONY

Ya beauty!

JONNY

Hullloooo!

TONY

What a team, eh?

JONNY

True grit, never say die. *(They're picking up their ripped-up season tickets.)*

TONY

Wait, haud on. The diddy's hit the side-netting.

JONNY

He's missed it?

(A pregnant pause before the collected pieces of season ticket are thrown away again.)

TONY

Are they no' the biggest bunch of diddies you've ever seen in your life?

JONNY

I'm never comin' back.

TONY

That's it!

JONNY

Finito!

TONY

The end.

(*Ninety minutes plus injury-time have come and gone. The players head off down the tunnel. The supporters head off into the night leaving Scottish football on the treatment table having its bruises attended to.*)

THE END

QUIZ TIME

1. Duncan Shearer?
2. Darren Jackson?
3. Duncan Shearer *and* Darren Jackson?
4. Why Ken McRobb?
5. Aren't Jim Leishman's poems crap?
6. Do *you* think they're funny?
7. That Paul Kane's got some coupon, hasn't he?
8. Dougie Donnelly's haircut, did he chicken out in the middle of getting a Gazza?
9. The Celtic away strip. Is that no' hellish?
10. Bill Leckie is only in his early thirties!?!?
11. How come Chic Charnley's real name is John?
12. Why does *Sportscene* get Eamonn Bannon in?
13. Why do fans buy flags at Hampden when the police always make you put them in the bin?
14. Why do the police pull up the wee boys with the flags but let those tanning the Buckfast ten yards away from them into the ground?
15. Is there not some law about bevvy and football?
16. That Graham Speirs fancies himself, eh?
17. How can journalists name Brian Laudrup as Player of the Year before the season's even started?
18. Whalt elver halperned do Tom Frerrie?

19. Now that scientists have proved it wasn't a goal then surely it would be reasonable to expect a replay of the '66 World Cup final?

20. You know how when Angus Simpson and Viv Lumsden, or Shereen or that other bloke on *Scotland Today* hand over to Jim Delahunt with a duff joke and he just sits there looking like a rabbit caught in the headlights? What's all that about?

AMAZING FACTS ABOUT SCOTTISH FOOTBALL

Glasgow Rangers were originally called Glasgow Shamrock but dropped the name in 1884 to avoid being labelled sectarian.

John Robertson of Hearts used to be six feet four inches tall but, following a human cannonball prank that went tragically wrong, his spine contracted to make him the height he is today.

The creators of the film *Batman Forever* came to Scotland and researched the lives of Maurice Johnston and Jim Farry before developing the villains Two-Face and The Riddler.

Craig Brown is not the father of Jock Brown but is in fact his brother. Other famous soccer brothers include Hugh and William McIlvanney, Jim McLean and Tommy McLean, Rangers and the Referees Committee.

A secret poll taken at the time revealed that 90 per cent of fans were in favour of the introduction of football ID cards. The main reasons being: 'When I'm blootered I can look at it and know who I um.'

We can exclusively reveal that Gerry McNee used to sport a goatee beard nearly twenty years before they were trendy. He only shaved it off when he got fed up with being constantly mistaken for Dr Who's arch enemy, The Master.

The Queen doesn't support Rangers and the Pope doesn't support Celtic; however, the Dalai Lama is a Clyde man and described Charlie Nicholas's move as a 'great signing for the Bully Wee'.

At a recent charity auction, Mark Hateley paid £10,000 for one of Arthur Montford's jackets. There is a strong rumour that he intends to wear it.

When Aberdeen won the European Cup-Winners Cup in 1983, they did it with Doug Rougvie in the team.

Fearing a repeat of the warlike 1994 Scottish Junior Cup final, the *Scotsport* commentary team was originally Gerry McNee with summaries from Raymond Baxter.

If Celtic (six times), Aberdeen (three times) and Dundee United (once) hadn't won the Premier League Championship then, this season, Rangers would be going for twenty-one in a row.

When Raith hit-man Ally Graham spotted his valuation in a Fantasy Football game – £400,000 – he complained to the newspaper in question. When the paper spotted their mistake, they apologised and amended the misprint. Ally is now valued at £40,000.

Originally developed to stop balls rolling down the Easter Road slope, square footballs were introduced to the Scottish scene in 1958. Slightly easier to control than the round ones, FIFA considered making them compulsory but the SFA protested that square balls would slow the game down too much so the plan was ditched.

Terry Christie called in mind-bender Jack Black to prepare him mentally for the slagging he takes for wearing that duffle coat.

Manchester United sell more players than Queen of the South sell pies.

1994

Only an Excuse? 1994
starred
JONATHAN WATSON and TONY ROPER
and was first performed at the Citizens' Theatre, Glasgow
on 20 September 1994

1994

ACT ONE

(Another show. Another swipe at our national obsession. Another selection of Richard Clayderman's favourite football chants tinkles through the PA system.

The music fades. 'Ah, now for the thunderclap,' think the veterans of the previous year's show; but they're wrong. The lights are still up and the audience are still clambering to their seats as the following important announcement is made.)

ANNOUNCER

Good evening, ladies and gentlemen, and welcome to tonight's performance of *Only an Excuse?*. As is customary in this theatre, would you now please be up-standing for the National Anthem.

(A few bars from 'God Save the Queen' but this suddenly switches to a tone-deaf duo singing in imperfect harmony.)

DUO

> We hate Jimmy Hill,
> He's a poof, he's a poof.
> We hate Jimmy Hill,
> He's a poof, he's a poof.
> We hate Jimmy Hill,
> He's a poof, he's a poof.

ANNOUNCER

> Thank you, ladies and gentlemen. Tonight's
> performance will now kick off.

> *(Those who fell for it and did stand up pretend they are
> only checking their seat number. But there is no time for
> scintillating debate on the musical/political/hysterical
> qualities of 'God Save the Queen', because before you can
> say 'I like the royal family, it's the hangers-on I can't
> stand', the theatre is plunged into darkness and our old
> friend the thunderclap heralds the arrival of a godlike
> voice.)*

WILLIAM McILVANNEY

> I have a dream that one day this nation will rise up
> and live out the meaning of its creed – that all players
> are created equal but some get paid more than others. I
> have a dream today! I have a dream that one day the
> supporters of this beautiful game will be judged not by
> the colour of their scarves but by the content of their
> carry-out bags. I have a dream today! I have a dream
> that one day the ethnic cleansing of our language will
> cease, the verbal atrocities will abate and the

grammatical terrors what they have brunged into wur mediums will be mollicated. I have a dream today! I have a dream that football of the people, for the people, by the people, shall not perish from this earth – but will only be available on Sky TV. I have a dream today! I have a dream today! I have a dream today! I have a dream today!

(The curtains have opened. A dim light on the set backdrop slowly grows brighter. What does that say? 'World Cup Albania 2006'? Explain. The voice on the mystical trannie does just that.)

COMMENTATOR

We've played two minutes of injury time in this, the eighteenth World Cup final. The match official, Clive Brooks from England, and what a match he's had, looks at his watch . . . and that's it, it's all over! The final score is Scotland three, the mighty Albania two – which means Scotland are World Champions *again!*

(Enter two futuristic Tartan Army foot soldiers celebrating Scotland's footballing glory.)

BOTH

Bonnie Scotland, Bonnie Scotland, we'll support you ever more . . . we'll support you ever more.

JONNY

Ho, ho, ho! Ya beauty!

TONY

Yesss!

JONNY

I cannae believe it, I just cannae believe it! We done it
in 1998, we done it in 2002 and, here, have we no'
went and done it again in 2006! It's pure magical.

TONY

I know, imagine Scotland winning the World Cup for
the third time in a row. I'm pure ecstatic so I am.

JONNY

Me too. In fact, I'm so happy I think I'm gonnae greet.

TONY

Me as well.

*(Arms around each other, they have a sentimental wee
greet to themselves, then they regain control of their
emotions.)*

JONNY

Awright, that's me, I'm awright now. I've had ma wee
greet.

TONY

I'm fine as well.

JONNY

It's funny when you think about it all the same
though, eh? I mean Scotland make us greet now
because they win everything but it's not that long ago
they used to make us greet because they were always
getting gubbed . . . gloriously, of course.

TONY

Ah, but that was back in the bad old days. That's when
Scotland were the only country in the world that used
to psyche *in* the opposition.

JONNY

Not any more, though, not any more. Now they fear
us like the Trojans feared the Greeks, like the Normans
feared the Vikings, like the Daleks feared . . . a
staircase.

TONY

And it's not just our international reputation that's
benefiting. I mean, look at the benefits that's benefited
the domestic game.

JONNY

Benefits? Like what? The only thing that would benefit
our league is a laxative. It's constipated, it needs some
movement. I mean, come on, twelve league
championships in a row . . . Partick Thistle's
domination is ruining the game.

TONY

Well, I said it at the time and I'll say it again now. Scottish football will rue the day that they allowed Silvio Berlusconi to buy the Jags.

JONNY

I suppose it's up to the other teams to mount a serious challenge.

TONY

Och, like who, for instance?

JONNY

Well, what about the Big Two?

TONY

Nah, Berwick will fall away and Montrose always bottle it against the Jags.

JONNY

Rangers?

TONY

Nah, they'll never do anything. Not with that signing policy of theirs.

JONNY

Oh come on, that's all in the past. After all, this is the year 2006 and Rangers have said they *will* sign a

Scottish Protestant . . . if they can find one who's good enough.

TONY

Ah, well, I'll believe that when I see it. But I'll tell you something: I think Celtic could surprise a few people this year. I reckon they could win something.

JONNY

Like what?

TONY

Promotion. That would be a big bonus for Tommy Burns in the year that the people of Kilmarnock finally lifted the contract on him.

JONNY

I suppose we could always turn our back on the senior game and follow the junior teams, like Kilwinning Rangers, the Weans of William, Glenafftheirheids or Auchinleck Bampot . . .

TONY

No. Junior football isn't the same since it was made compulsory for the players to wear crash helmets.

JONNY

I think the authorities overreacted with that ruling.

TONY

Well, the chairman of the disciplinary committee felt that there was no place in the modern game for lack of discipline and what Mr Charles Charnley says goes.

JONNY

It is still amazing all the same, when you think about it – Scotland dominating world football.

TONY

No' just the world, *Europe* as well. Hey, do you remember the very first time we won the European Championships way back in 1996? Beat England 7–6 in the final at Wembley – after being 6–0 down at half-time.

JONNY

So, was that when Scottish football underwent the revolution that made it what it is today – the best in the world?

TONY

No, that was 1994.

JONNY

1994? What was significant about that year? I mean, anything out of the ordinary happen? Anything totally unbelievable?

TONY

Hibs beat Hearts.

JONNY

Any political turmoil?

TONY

The Monklands by-election.

JONNY

Any religious turmoil?

TONY

The Monklands by-election.

JONNY

And what about the media? Was it them that led the Scottish football revolution back in 1994?

TONY

Well, there's one way to find out.

(*Blackout. Sportscene music.*)

THE VOICE OF JOCK BROWN

And there it is, the final whistle. Dundee United have beaten Rangers to lift the Scottish Cup.

(Lights up. Music fades.)

DOUGIE DONNELLY

Dougie Donnelly here. Hello and welcome to a very hushed, a very depressed Hampden Park, where the fans have now gone off to ponder, to reflect and to throw stones at each other's buses after a totally forgettable Scottish Cup final. It really was rubbish, wasn't it, Chick?

CHICK YOUNG

Ho! Ho! Ho! Dougie, only I'm not laughing because this was, make no bones about it, a total tragedy for Scottish football. Because if teams don't start lying down to Glasgow Rangers, Murray's mighty mazongas will become Italian and join the Italian league, or become Bundies and join the Bundesliga, and that will be the end of the road for Scottish football.

DOUGIE DONNELLY

So do you think they will leave *en masse*, Chick?

CHICK YOUNG

Hold on, Dougie. I never said anything about them becoming Catholics.

DOUGIE DONNELLY

But, eh, let's not take anything away from Dundee United though . . . oh, bugger it, let's take everything away from Dundee United – I mean Rangers really

124

just handed it to them, didn't they, Chick?

CHICK YOUNG

Absolutely in a totally total sense, Dougie, and casting
no blame or pointing no finger at anyone in particular,
Dave McPherson should be shot, bayoneted, hung up,
drawn and quartered and fed to the crows . . . or, even
worse, sold back to Hearts.

DOUGIE DONNELLY

And, eh, Craig Brewster's goal, Chick . . . surely that
could have been disallowed for . . . offside, dangerous
play or, at the very least, unsportsmanlike behaviour?

CHICK YOUNG

Not only that, Dougie, but when Christian Dailly
knocked the ball across goal, he was definitely
interfering with destiny. But for my money, the goal
should have been disallowed on the grounds that Ally
Maxwell wisnae ready.

DOUGIE DONNELLY

And what about the referee, Chick, Douglas Hope?

CHICK YOUNG

Douglas Hope rhymes with 'Pope'. Rest my case,
Dougie.

DOUGIE DONNELLY

Ah, that's quite disturbing, Chick, and all the more

remarkable to think that that sort of thing can go unchecked in, what is after all, don't forget, a Protestant country. And talking of which, I think we can go over now to Walter Smith . . . can we? . . . no, we can't . . . Chick, I . . . yes, we can . . . well, Walter Smith is with . . . no one.

WALTER SMITH

Obviously, I'm particularly disappointed in particular with the result, at the present moment, particularly in view of the fact that it ended the dream of a historic double treble which we weren't even thinking about. Obviously, I don't think this is particularly the time to criticise the team and particularly to be suggesting that they are finished, particularly as we've still got some great players at Castle Greyskull. When *he's* on his game, Richard Gough is a world-beater; and when *he's* on the bevvy, David Robertson is a panel-beater.

DOUGIE DONNELLY

Walter, heartfelt sympathies from all of us here at the BBC sports department, the wreath is on its way.

WALTER SMITH

Thanks, Dougie.

DOUGIE DONNELLY

Well, Walter Smith, as ever putting on a brave smile in the face of an unjust defeat. But what about the man of the moment, the hero of the day. I'm sure he's got something to say and I'm sure we want to hear it but, sadly, we can't find Coisty so here's Chick with Ivan Golac.

CHICK YOUNG

Yes, Dougie, this is totally me, far-out Chick Young, inviting you to tune in, turn on and drop out of your chair in total astonishment because this is the dawning of the Age of Unitedus, the times they are a-changing-room and this tangerine dream is no bad trip for the man floating up from the floor right now, Ivan Golac.

(Ivan Golac, joint in hand, floats into view.)

IVAN GOLAC

Hey, Chicko, chill out, easy take it. Ah! Look at the flowers, all those colours, so beautiful. Look around you. Life is, you know, for to enjoy and to win things, you know, because let me tell you, there's nothing to beat the sweet smell of success . . . unless it's a sweet smell of the wacky-baccy.

CHICK YOUNG

Ivan, what do you recall about the goal that won Dundee United the cup?

IVAN GOLAC

I remember Christian Dailly chasing back for the ball that is loose, yeah? Then it comes across goal and a giant psychedelic giraffe knocks it into the goal.

CHICK YOUNG

Ivan, once again, congratulations and thanks for *ruining* Cup-final day for everyone in the Scottish media except Hugh Keevins, Davy Provan and, of course, Dougie Donnelly's son, Dick.

DICK DONNELLY

Yes, Dick Donnelly here at a rather delirious, delightful fandabbiedozie, drunken stooshie in a normally dreich, dour, dull, dire, deadly Dundee where I'm sure Golac's Gallus Glories will be really rubbing this victory into the faces of Tayside rivals Duffy's Dens Park Diddies – in a light-hearted way, of course. There have been rumours of a Tannadice tiff between Ivan Golac and Jim McLean and I'm sure Ivan's Cup-final record, one win out of one appearance, will be compared with Jim's hee-haw out of six the next time they are having a square go – in a light-hearted way, of course.

CHICK YOUNG

Who's a clever Dick, then? You must be very proud of your boy, Dougie.

DOUGIE DONNELLY

Proud is not the word, Chick . . . is it? . . . Yes, it is . . . No, it isn't . . . But never mind, let's chase away those Cup-final true blues with a quick look back at last season where there was just so much happening . . . Was there? . . . No, there wasn't . . . Yes, there was. Broadwood Stadium at Cumbernauld has two clubs

It's Pittodrie for thrills, and as Aberdeen lay siege to the halfway line, this fired-up Dons fan can hardly contain his excitement

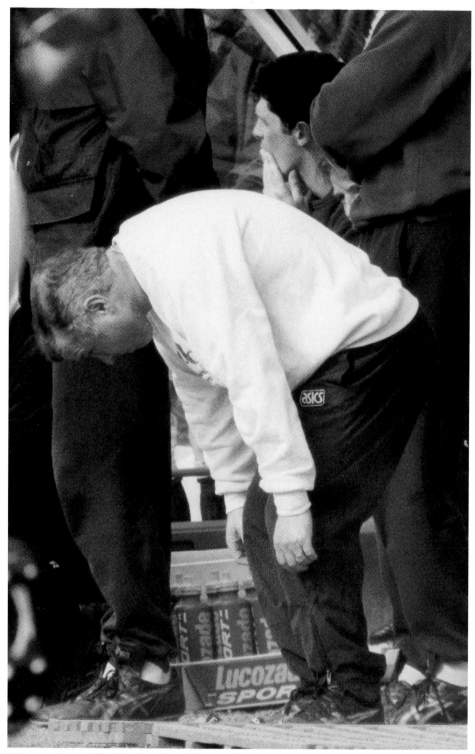

It's party time at Tynecastle where Tommy McLean celebrates another successful season for Hearts by doing the hokey-kokey

Food for thought: Has the traditional greasy pie had its day? Catering staff at Rugby Park might agree as Kilmarnock boss Alex Totten leads the fans in a rousing chorus of 'I feel like chicken tonight'

Mayfest. And Firhill is the unlikely venue for Gerry Collins' acting debut as he takes on the Jack Nicholson role in a John Lambie production of *One Flew Over the Cuckoo's Nest* entitled *One Flew Over the Pigeon Loft*

Following the outcry over the new Scotland international team strip, more complaints are expected over the design for the new Scotland international cap

The SFA are looking into accusations that our match officials are taking it all too lightly, following an incident at a packed Kilbowie Park when the referee disallowed a goal because he was unsighted

Following his decision to wear his hooded tracksuit back-to-front, Davey Dodds has once again been allowed to train with the rest of the lads

Diamonds are forever! Memories of Broomfield's bisexual ball-player come flooding back as we remember the day Justin Fashanu modelled the new Airdrie 'Have it Away' strip

Falkirk chairman George Fulston can hardly contain his delight as he enjoys the lavish comforts of one of the recently opened Executive Boxes at Brockville Stadium

'The SAS is the only team I've ever wanted to play for.' Fans' favourite Maurice Johnston models his own exclusive Falkirk away strip specially designed for his trips to Celtic Park . . . and Ibrox Stadium . . . and Tynecastle . . . and Firhill . . . and Victoria's . . .

playing there now, and when you consider that not so long ago there was only some auld coos walking about the park, well, it's perhaps not so remarkable that Airdrie feel quite at home there. And trendy Ayr boss, Simon Stainrod, grew a beard. I suppose if you're going to act the goat you might as well look like one. Meanwhile Celtic collapsed by instalments in a catalogue of disasters.

CHICK YOUNG

A catalogue indeed, Dougie, the board made an *Argos* of it. And to see this once-proud club so well and truly in the grubber . . . highlight of the season for me, Dougie.

DOUGIE DONNELLY

Yes, but things had to change at Celtic Park, Chick, and sadly perhaps, they did. Bringing to an end a great tradition of dithering dogma and devout paranoia.

WILLIAM McILVANNEY

The Berlin Wall had fallen, communism had collapsed and soon the last great bastion of intransigence would also crumble. The wind of change blowing through Celtic Park caused a rift. The families fell out, the minging dynasties lost their grip. Morale had, in the past, dropped lower than David Syme's trousers but now, as a new dawn beckoned, players past and present felt the need to become involved and make their viewpoint clear – Danny McGrain wasn't one of them.

DANNY McGRAIN

It was unbelievable. Horrible, terrible, miserable, and any other -ibles you care to mention. But now I think it's time to give Lou Macari some support and not be too critical of the fact he took two canteen women with him on a trip to Ireland – after all, he's tried everyone else in the centre of the defence. Of course, it's easy for me to say what I think, but it must have been difficult for players who were still playing for Celtic . . . *and* for Charlie Nicholas, too, who spoke out secondly as a Celtic supporter but firstly as a player facing his jotters. But, er, that's all in the past and I'm sure all Celtic supporters are now more optimistic and I think that's all down to one man – that's the bank manager who said you're getting no more money. And Brian Dempsey done good too.

BRIAN DEMPSEY

What we have today is a situation of which we are not quite sure, for the purpose of who knows what, in the realms of where, when and why; but what I do know is who, and that who is him, my great wee mate, Fergus McCann, who prepared thoroughly for his coming to Celtic Park – he spent two months in the Coatbridge Time Capsule. So, without further ado, let's meet Fergus because I know there are a load of questions stoating around about the wee man – like how long will he be here? How much will he invest? When is he going to get a bunnet that fits him?

FERGUS McCANN *(initially looking the wrong way; he realises this and turns round to face the audience)*

> A McCann's gotta do what a McCann's gotta do, so, as from today, the Celtic manager is no longer *Mr* Luigi Macari.
>
> Now, regarding a replacement, I have – *we* have – a number of people in mind. Tommy Burns strikes me as a first-class candidate for the job but obviously he's contracted to Kilmarnock so it would be unethical for me to suggest to him to pack in his job and come and work for us. So if you're listening, Tom, please ignore this statement, my mobile number is 18.88.71.71.71.

WILLIAM McILVANNEY

> In the end, Fergus didn't sing the blues because, surprise, surprise, Tommy returned to the 'Tic while Killie faced the stark reality that Billy was off too. But in football the dust never settles on a story until it's going for fifty pence at Bargain Books. There are two sides to every tale and just as every dog has its day, every ex-director has its publishing deal. Michael Kelly's account of the end of Timilisation as he knew it promised to be a book with lots of words in it and worthy of serious intellectual discussion.

> *(Jingle: Radio Scotland's* Sportsound.*)*

BOB CRAMPSEY

> Good afternoon, Bob Crampsey here. Welcome to *Sportsound.* I've just been speaking to Michael Kelly, who was expounding the theory that Robert Burns was

rubbish and that the only reason folk go on about him is because he was a masonic Proddie, while I was waxing lyrical about the sheer poetic poetry and almost balletic beauty of another of Scotland's sons. But I am prepared to accept that Crawford Baptie isn't everyone's idea of a footballer nor, perhaps, is Michael Kelly everyone's idea of an author, but I've an awful feeling we're about to find that out.

MICHAEL KELLY

Paradise Lost, £10.99 from all good book stores, by Dr Michael Kelly aged forty-six and a half.

'What though the field be lost, all is not lost the unconquerable will, and study of revenge immortal hate and courage never to submit or yield,' I quipped to Jack McGinn as he brought in my tea that spring morning.

'Better to reign in hell than serve in heaven,' rasped Tom Grant as he realised there were no green-wrapped Penguins left in the barrel.

Suddenly the door burst open and I was confronted by the cousin from hell, Kevin 'Mad Dog' Kelly.

KEVIN KELLY

Michael, I am fair beeling, so I am –

MICHAEL KELLY

– he blasted. But why Kevin?' I mused rationally, 'is there something untoward?'

KEVIN KELLY

Och, Mike, look at the books! We're in a shambles.
Please sort out the mess we're in and lead us all into a
bright new future. You're the only man for the job,
man for the job . . . man for the job.

MICHAEL KELLY

As all the others agreed with Kevin, I felt humbled,
but resolved not to let my humility get in the way of
my duty – nay, my destiny – to lead this club into a
glorious epoch. It was then that I told Michelle Pfeiffer
to away and gie us peace.

BOB CRAMPSEY

Thanks, Michael, sounds fascinating. I must remember
to forget to get a copy; but moving on from a petty
boy to a pretty boy, Gordon Smith is with Jim Baxter.

GORDON SMITH

Jim, lookin' great, feelin' like a million dollars – but
enough about me. How are you?

JIM BAXTER

I feel great, marvellous. I got my first kidney on the
Friday then I got another one on the Sunday. Wee
Jinky says, 'By God, you must've sank some amount of
bevvy on the Saturday.'

GORDON SMITH

Is that right, Jim *(looks in mirror)* . . . What a shag.

JIM BAXTER

But ken this, if I could go back to the beginning again, the first thing I would do is get myself an agent.

BILL McMURDO

May I be allowed to speak? McMurdo here. The Bill. And the first thing I would say is that agenting is all about looking after players – like recently when I had to confront the unacceptable face of Scottish football: Stevie Fulton. In securing this player's move to Falkirk, I performed two acts of kindness. Stevie's pace takes some of the pressure off the midfield and Stevie's face takes some of the pressure off Yogi Hughes. But from one Billy Boy to another: they'll be laughing in the streets of Raith at Jiminy Nicholl.

JIMINY NICHOLL

C'mere, there's more, there's more. Have you heard about Craig Brown? Craig Brown, manager of Scotland. When he heard Scotland were playing the Faroes he flew out on a spying mission to Egypt. No, no, no. C'mere, there's more. What about Helen Liddell? She's complaining to the Vatican about the strength of the Buckfast wine. But the Vatican will do nothing. That's the only method of contraception they allow. No, no, no. C'mere, there's more. Lorena Bobbit: Radio Clyde have hired her to take charge of their phone-in. They'd heard that she's good at cutting off pricks. That's it, there's no more.

134

WILLIAM McILVANNEY
But, ultimately, the joke is on us. We stand on the shoreline of sanity watching our hopes and dreams carried on the crest of a radio-wave crashing against the rambling rocks of the irrational as every week, without fail, we dial FM for murder.

FIRST VOICE
Hi, this is Craig Brown . . .

SECOND VOICE
Hello, Mark Hateley here . . .

THIRD VOICE
Hello, I'm Paul McStay . . .

FOURTH VOICE
Hi, Richard Gough here . . .

FIFTH VOICE
John f***ing Lambie speaking . . .

SIXTH VOICE
I'm Andy Goram . . .

SEVENTH VOICE
This is Ally McCoist MBE . . .

EIGHTH VOICE

Hello, my name is . . . er . . . er . . . gie us a clue then.
What? Oh, aye, right, Duncan Ferguson.

ANNOUNCER

All the big names are on Clyde . . . and Hugh Keevins.

HUGH KEEVINS

In my opinion, and I stress it is only an opinion, the
problem lies *not* with the league set-up, *not* with the
press, *not* with the much-maligned media in which I
myself include me, and *not*, I repeat *not*, with the wee
boys who say 'Can I watch your motor, mister?'. No,
for me the problem is, quite simply, to be or not to be
summer football. That is the question, is it not, Derek
Johnstone?

DEREK JOHNSTONE

Well, fair dos, this is what it's all about. I happen to
think summer football is a bad idea because that's
when I go my holidays.

CHICK YOUNG

Hear hear, there there, and so say all of me. Leaving
aside the snow and ice and frost and slush and rain
and sleet and hailstones and blizzards and mud, you've
got to ask yourself, is it really that bad? Dick Donnelly.

DICK DONNELLY

Well, I hold the view that it would make, sadly, not

one bit of difference because these conditions Chick has just described are typical of Dundee's summer weather anyway. Isn't that right, Davy Provan?

DAVY PROVAN

Hello Dick, well Chick, yes Derek, too true Hugh, Davy Provan here. If it was only those conditions Chick described then it would probably be okay, but there's fog as well. I remember last season being at a Celtic *v* Aberdeen match when the fog was so thick that Archie MacPherson couldn't see what was happening, therefore his commentary didn't make any sense. So, no change there. And talking of changes, there have certainly been plenty of those south of the border, down Liverpool way.

JONATHAN PEARCE

Goa-a-a-l-l-l-l! Bristol City one, Liverpool nil . . . what now for Graeme Souness?

GRAEME SOUNESS

Can I just say something here? Yeah, for sure, it was difficult, but I have reached the conclusion that the best thing for the club is if I abdicate. My thoughts might change but right now I just want to get as far away from football as possible – so yes, there is some foundation to the rumour that I'm thinking of buying Hearts.

DEREK JOHNSTONE

Davy! That is a shocker!

DAVY PROVAN

Derek, that is a *quality* shocker. Now I know there were those who found Graeme Souness arrogant, smug, big-headed, self-centred, proud almost beyond belief and in it only for himself, but I totally disagree with that – I never found him smug. In the meantime, let's bring in Graeme's friend and rival, Alex Ferguson.

ALEX FERGUSON

Ah well, as a football manager myself, I take no pleasure in seeing another manager – or even Graeme Souness – lose his job. Some people say he was wrong to leave Rangers but he'd made too many enemies in Scotland so he had to move south . . . and make some enemies down here. Okay, so things certainly went bad for him on the park but the team's results did create a new look for Liverpool. Red socks, red shorts, red shirts and red faces. Isn't that right, Denis Law?

DENIS LAW

Well, you know, as I say, for me, the problem area for Liverpool was between the sticks, you know, the goalkeeper's position, the number-one jersey, where, to me, the only competition between Grobbelaar and James was to see who could have the stupidest hairstyle. But you know, as I say, even I was surprised that he couldn't just go out and get a real goalkeeper given England's great tradition of ball-handlers, you know, like Gordon Banks, Peter Shilton, Gerald Sinstadt . . . you know?

ALEX FERGUSON

Ah, but Denis, he signed Dicks.

DENIS LAW

Excuse me, Alex, but I don't like to hear footballers being referred to in that way. I'm sorry.

ALEX FERGUSON

No, no. *Julian* Dicks. He signed Julian Dicks from West Ham.

DENIS LAW

Of course he did, yes, he signed Dicks to stiffen the defence and Ruddock to stiffen everybody else, you know, but what they lacked upfront in the midfield of the back four was a schemer – like a Kevin Keegan on the right side, or an Ian Callaghan on the left side, or a Barry Grant on the *Brookside*. But to know the *real* Graeme Souness I think you'd have to have played with him – isn't that right, Willie Miller?

WILLIE MILLER

Well, I happen to think everybody has the wrong idea about Souness. I remember back in the 1982 World Cup in Spain. Alan Hansen and I decided to do our bit to end the Cold War by gifting Russia a goal. Now I knew Graeme was angry at us but he was a true professional. He never criticised us, he never slagged us, and he never spoke to us ever again. Did you ever witness that side to his nature, Kenny Dalglish?

KENNY DALGLISH

Could be. Could no' be. Maybes aye. Maybes . . . maybes we're too critical of Graeme Souness. He spent something like thirty million. Okay, it didn't work out. All I can say is, personally speaking, from my point of view, it cannae be easy operating in the transfer market with such paltry amounts of money.

DEREK JOHNSTONE

Well, sorry to interrupt you there, Kenny. Derek Johnstone here. And to me that's what's wrong with the game today. Irresponsible spending by lucky rich bastards has grossly inflated the transfer market. But the last word has to go with Graeme Souness.

GRAEME SOUNESS

Yeah, for sure, it was a tough time for me but, as the *Daily Record* shows, I took the blows and did it my way. Regrets? Well, I've had a few . . .

Rangers? Well, my entire time spent there will probably always come down to that one signing and all the ugliness it caused, but to this day I stick by my decision to bring Davy Dodds to Ibrox.

The future? Well, I've had time to think, time to mellow, and yeah, for sure, I'm a changed man because Kipling *was* right – you've got to treat success and failure the same . . . studs on the shins early doors, they'll never bother you again.

DEREK JOHNSTONE

So the leopard can change its stripes after all. Graeme

Souness switches from crippling to Kipling – different class. I like an exceedingly good cake myself.

WILLIAM McILVANNEY

The Reds showed no mercy to their once-proud war chief. Now the media tribe moved off to ambush settlers on the soccer frontier, to wipe out wagon trains of would-be wonder boys. The tactics never changed, the war-cry never wavered . . . bury my heart at wounded McNee. White man speak with forked tongue.

(*Blackout. Blast of* Scotsport *jingle.*)

JIM WHITE

Hi, Jim White here and you've just made the best possible start to match day by tuning into *Scotsport Extra Whine*. Okay, hit me with those exclusives, Gerry.

GERRY McNEE

Yes, Jim, and first up I can exclusively reveal that FIFA are set to investigate the alleged miracle properties of the new Predator football boots. It is claimed that these boots could make Aberdeen's Brian Irvine hit the ball *straight*.

JIM WHITE

Miracle indeed. Anything else, Gerry?

GERRY McNEE

It seems nothing can de-rail the Ibrox flute bandwagon. Such is their confidence that the Rangers supporters can even cope with their fanzine, the *Daily Record*, revealing the shock news that King Billy was gay. The resourceful Rangers faithful have simply changed their battle songs to 'Hello, hello, sailor, we are the Billy Boys', 'The cry was no suspenders' and 'The sash and matching twinset my father wore'.

JIM WHITE

Go on yourself, big man. Season 1993–94. Some classic exclusives from Gerry McNee.

GERRY McNEE

Yes, Jim, and now some news involving Celtic's nursery club, Motherwell. My sources inform me that early next season the Parkhead club will sign the Steelmen's midfield star, Phil O'Donnell.

JIM WHITE

What a tragedy. How do you know that, Gerry?

GERRY McNEE

Through my sources.

JIM WHITE

Sure. And did Darlinda tell you anything else, Gerry?

GERRY McNEE

Yes. She said . . . er . . . my *sources* said that Scotland
will open their European campaign with a 2–0 victory
over Finland.

JIM WHITE

Big wowee, Gerry. I mean, Finland are mince.

GERRY McNEE

Yes, but they will beat them 2–0 *away* from home.

JIM WHITE

A 2–0 victory *in* Finland should set us up nicely for a
disaster against the Faroes – right, Gerry?

GERRY McNEE

Well, unfortunately, my half-hour session with my
sources was up then, Jim, so I have no idea what's
going to happen but, rest assured, I will continue to
make out that I do. So watch this space.

JIM WHITE

Well done, Gerry, that needed saying. Great exclusives
this week, Gerry.

GERRY McNEE

Yes, well, naturally, Jim, being sports editor I get all
the big stories, but that doesn't mean there isn't a place
for Paul Cooney, who'll be along with all the crappy
stuff later.

JIM WHITE

Sure. Okay, remember keep those stupid calls coming in. The number to dial is 1.6.9.0. – 1.6.9.0. – 1.6.9.0. And once we've got someone on the line who's comprehensible, we'll put you through to one of our panel of experts who are Davie Cooper, who used to play for Rangers and that's good enough for me; Graham Spiers of the *Smartarse on Sunday;* and Donald Findlay QC RFC FTP, who is simply the best. Donald, while we're waiting for one of the lads from the office to nip outside and phone us up with a bad East Coast accent banning the Celtic support from Ibrox – a victory for practical presbyterianism although you can't help but feel sorry for the ordinary decent Celtic scum, if indeed there is such a thing, Donald?

DONALD FINDLAY

Ah, yes. I have heard tales of such, but in my vast experience of life, the law and the after-dinner-speaking circuit, I have yet to uncover evidence of the existence of such a thing amongst the Protestantly challenged.

JIM WHITE

All the same, Donald, Celtic have protested strongly about this ban and you have to say . . . how *dare* they!

DONALD FINDLAY

Well, put it down to Proddie intuition, Jim, but we thought they might moan and whine about it so we did offer them an alternative solution – away back to

Rome! But you know what these people are like, Jim,
always whingeing on about potato famines and John F.
Kennedy and twelve in a row.

JIM WHITE

Twelve in a row?

DONALD FINDLAY

Nine league championships for Celtic, three
Eurovision song contests for Ireland.

JIM WHITE

Donald, you're a lawyer, you work in a courthouse.
You must have met *lots* of baddies.

DONALD FINDLAY

Yes, I will admit that a lot of my time is spent mixing
with people of dubious morality but, to be honest,
Jim, if you don't mind, I'd rather not talk about the
Rangers players.

JIM WHITE

Great answers. What a character – Donald Findlay. A
man on the level, a man who mingles with the
bluenoses, the back-scratchers and the funny
handshakers – and he has a job with Rangers, too.
Gerry?

GERRY McNEE

Yes, and just for the record I happen to think that

David Murray has got it absolutely right with this ban. These neds must be stopped. There is no place in our stands for unruly, nasty, violent, foul-mouthed, loutish thuggery. Let's keep this where it belongs – *on* the pitch.

JIM WHITE

The voice of reason: Gerry McNee.

GERRY McNEE

And while I'm on my high horse, what about Jim Farry? I can exclusively reveal that I don't like him. There is no place in Scottish football for such a homologated promulgator of verbosity.

JIM WHITE

Not only that, Gerry, but he uses big words too.

GERRY McNEE

Make no mistake. We are living in a dictatorship. The Godfarry is running football and that can't be right, because after all – that's *my* job.

JIM WHITE

Sieg heil, Gerry. *Scotsport, Scotsport, über alles.*

(*Blackout.* Scotsport *music.*)

146

WILLIAM McILVANNEY

Scotland. Football's twilight zone, a soccer tale of mystery and lack of imagination. Those who forget their past are destined to repeat it and we have to come full circle only to discover that we are a circle of fools.

DOUGIE DONNELLY

And welcome back. Dougie Donnelly reminding you, in case you've just joined us, that the final score in the Scottish Cup final was Dundee United one (jammy, fluky goal), Rangers nil (no luck on the day). But that's not the end of football this summer because coming up next month we've got the *big* one. Chick, it's fourteen inches and weighs eleven pounds –

CHICK YOUNG

– thanks very much, Dougie.

DOUGIE DONNELLY

Ha, ha. No, no, no. The *World Cup*, Chick . . . and I wonder what team from the Netherlands are you tipping to win the competition?

CHICK YOUNG

Correct, Dougie. I'm going for the Fathers of William. Yourself?

DOUGIE DONNELLY

Well, I'm going for Ireland, so good luck to Jack and

the lads. And from Chick and me, have a good summer and see you soon. Goodnight.

CHICK YOUNG
Cheers.

(Sportscene *theme. Bits of paper shuffling. Music stops. They're 'off air'.)*

CHICK YOUNG
You're going for Ireland then?

DOUGIE DONNELLY
Aye, that'll be right.

(Blackout, *complete and instantaneous. By the time the house lights come on, the curtains have been drawn shut and the players are already in their dressing-room having their half-time talk.)*

HALF-TIME

END OF ACT ONE

HALF-TIME ENTERTAINMENT

WRITE TO SOCCERBIZ SAM, THE MAN WHO KNOWS HEE-HAW

Dear Sam,
Is Celtic's John Hughes related to Arnold Schwarzenegger?
Not only do they look alike but they've got the same accent.
Casey, Skinflats.

Sam says . . .
John's a winner, he'll do well at Celtic.

Dear Sam,
Settle an argument, there's a blood feud resting on this. Did
Mark Hateley used to be in that television series *Kung Fu?*
Insane, Carstairs.

Sam says . . .
Mark's a winner, he'll do well at Rangers.

Dear Sam,
See how Paul Elliot sued Dean Saunders for a tackle that
ruined his career, well, how come he didn't sue the barber
that gave him the haircut that ruined his head?
Taylor, Glasgow.

Sam says . . .
Paul's a winner, he'll do well blethering on the telly.

Dear Sam,
Some gen please on Hibs dish Willie Miller.

Desperate, Leith.

Sam says . . .
Willie was born a few years ago and plays football for Hibs. His real name is William and he is *not* the same Willie Miller who used to play and boss Aberdeen.

Dear Sam,
Why is *The Wee Red Book* called *The Wee Red Book*? Surely it should be called *The Wee Red and White with a Few Black Bits Book*?

Obsessively Pedantic, Kilsyth.

Sam says . . .
The Wee Red Book's a winner and there's no place for your sort of racism in football.

OLD FIRM FANTASY FOOTBALL

Select your fantasy Old Firm teams from the lists of players linked with both clubs during the close season (but surprisingly didn't join – at least prior to publication!).

Celtic

Marc Degryse	Paul Bernard
Dimitri Radchenko	Stefan Chapuisat
Billy McKinlay	Gary Smith
Gordan Petric	Darren Jackson
Kevin Gallacher	Owen Coyle
Paulo Futre	John Robertson
Alain Sutter	Ian Wright
Neil McCann	Darko Pancev
Oleg Salenko	Peter Beagrie
Rod Wallace	Theo Snelders
Bo Hansen	Stevey Crawford
Norrie McWhirter	Shaka Hislop
David Ginola	Chris Waddle

Rangers

Florin Raduciou
Stevey Crawford
Jorge Cadette
Tomas Skuhravy
Ruud Gullit
Dennis Bergkamp
Jurgen Klinsmann
Nelson Mandela
Jesus Christ
God
Michael Laudrup
Hugh Laudrup
Bert Laudrup
Theo Snelders

Franz Beckenbauer
Albert Einstein
Damon Hill
Pete Sampras
Alexander the Great
Derek the Not Bad
Jim Morrison
Elvis Presley
Sir Stanley Matthews
Bodo Illgner
The Alexander Brothers
Lassie
Robbie out of Take That

WHO'S BETTER, WHO'S BEST?

Soccer celebrities name their top five players of all time.

Archie MacPherson
1. Brian Laudrup
2. Brian Laudrup
3. Brian Laudrup
4. Brian Laudrup
5. Brian Laudrup

Chick Young
1. Graeme Souness
2. Barry Lavety
3. Rikki Gillies
4. Me
5. Pele

Bill McMurdo
1. George Best
2. Maurice Johnston
3. John Knox
4. Scottie McClue
5. Her Most Glorious Britannic Majesty, Queen Elizabeth II

Andy Roxburgh
1. Xanthiedjavicz (Croatia)
2. Dzasersdfghlou (Latvia)
3. Duytrasdertyblo (Belarus)
4. Quelsdertroghy (Estonia)
5. Zoarthshasdertyoishretyshnmbofuth (Greenland)

Bernard Tapie
1. Garry Owen
2. Newsboy
3. Klondyke
4. Meridian
5. Ally McCoist

Eric Cantona
1. Rimbaud
2. Rambo
3. Joe Bugner
4. Bruce Lee
5. Les Kellet

Joe Miller
1. Roy of the Rovers
2. Raven on the Wing
3. The Cannonball Kid
4. Alf Tupper
5. Biggles

Judge Dredd
1. Terry Hurlock
2. Gregor Stevens
3. Willie Johnston
4. Duncan Ferguson
5. Willie McVie

Alan McInally
1. My mate Lothar
2. My best pal Brian
3. My old mucker Kenny
4. My good china Roberto
5. My great amigo Ruud

Dick Donnelly
1. Sanny Shaw (Dundee 1934)
2. 'Stoorie' Burns (United 1900)
3. Fat Boabby Soutar (Dundee 1824)
4. Eckie Cox (United 1769)
5. Noel Blake

1994

ACT TWO

(The curtains open quietly. A now-familiar voice sets the scene for Act Two.)

WILLIAM McILVANNEY

They say things work in cycles. If this is true then Scottish football's cycle is a Raleigh Chopper: outdated, outmoded, outstandingly deficient when compared to the mountain-bike mentality of the continentals. We no longer stand at the edge of the abyss – we are the abyss. We no longer shoot ourselves in the foot – we blow our entire legs off. So who is going to save our game? Who has the answers? Out of the mouths of babes and fools and our own, our very own fans.

(Suddenly two spotlights hit the stage and there they are, a Celtic fan and a Rangers fan, separated only by fifteen feet of stage and three hundred years of suspicion.)

SEAN

Sean Lourdes. Half-Scottish, half-Irish, half-Roman,

half-baked theories on how the Dobs are to blame for all the world's ills. Fifth dan altarboy, ninja passkeeper also known as Seany, Lourdesy or, by my confirmation name, Peter Grant.

BOYNE

Boyne Schoenberg Syme. Half-Scottish, half-Dutch, half and a half pint please. Imperial wizard, grand worshipful master, lay preacher also known as Truth Defender, Scourge of the Tims or, by my adopted Lakota Sioux name, Dances with Flutes.

SEAN

I just got back from the World Cup, so time to catch up with the latest headlines . . . Following the Rod Stewart incident at Hampden Park, Kilmarnock are set to follow Celtic and introduce lookalikes to entertain their fans. They hope to introduce this development when Celtic visit Rugby Park and are currently looking for the following lookalikes: King Billy, John Knox and Martin Luther.

BOYNE

Rangers are no longer interested in Alan McLaren and have targeted Prince Charles as the man to strengthen their defence. This shock move comes after Rangers' European scouts saw recent photies of the prince in a French magazine and were very impressed with his tackle.

SEAN

The radio broadcaster who had been missing since the weekend has been found hungry but safe in Govan. Derek Johnstone had gone there on Saturday to look for 'The Big Picnic'.

BOYNE

Following the recent revelation that Celtic players have been taking tablets originally developed for horses, Albion Rovers have denied they've been taking tablets originally developed for donkeys.

SEAN

Despite being dropped from the first team, Maurice Johnston has said that he will fight for his place at Hearts. So he's challenged Tommy McLean to a square go.

BOYNE

With the successful introduction of a lookalike Elvis Presley and Rod Stewart to play to the fans, Celtic are now looking for lookalike Billy McNeills and Danny McGrains to play in their defence.

SEAN

Just in case you were wondering, I was over supporting Ireland. Just got back so I've got a bit of catching up to do although I've got an awful feeling I've missed everything and yet I've missed nothing. What is the gossip? What's the Hampden roar? I'm feart to ask.

BOYNE

America was a rubbish place. You couldnae get a copy of the *Rangers News* anywhere so, naturally, I'm not quite up to date with world affairs, right?

But I suppose it was worth while goin', no' just for the magic of seeing Holland gub Ireland but also for broadening the narrowness of my mind. To be honest, I thought, 'What can they show us, what can Gloryland teach Grubberland?' Quite a lot as it turned out.

WILLIAM McILVANNEY

World Cup USA was a total, unmitigated disaster for all those cynics who had confidently predicted a soccatastrophe. For this tournament was truly a celebration of the beautiful game. The television coverage captured it all. The tension, the pressure, the breakaway. The jinking and weaving, the speed, the swerves – then the audience got fed-up with O.J. Simpson and tuned into the football.

There was a new coating on the ball. What could it be? Against Holland, Pat Bonner provoked allegations it was Tefal.

And then there was England's moment of glory – Maradona failed his dope test. And there to offer his expertise on drug abuse, Ally McLeod.

ALLY McLEOD *(holding up his medals)*

I've got them back! Ach, well, tremendous, absolutely delighted, y'know. So somebody failed a dope test? Big deal, we did that ages ago. Ach, well, contrary to what everybody says about back then, the spirits in the Argentine were brilliant. I mean, the tequila would've

blown yir heid aff. But, ach, well, I'm just delighted,
'cause, I mean, as the song says, 'Don't greet for me
Argentina' . . . and it didnae – it pissed itself laughing.
Ach, well, I mean, that was then and this is now, and
you have to wonder about Maradona because that was
some drugs cocktail he took, by the way. Although
personally speaking, I think it was a set-up. I think the
chemist set them up and wee Diego downed them,
y'know? Maybe you'd be better speaking to somebody
who knows him, like Ossie Ardiles.

OSSIE ARDILES

To be perfectly honest, I know he try drastic measure
to lose weight like exercise but when this not work he
start injecting Lean Cuisines and snorting Slimfast.
But to be perfectly honest I am very sad because I had
hoped that after good World Cup, Diego would come
to England, settle down, learn the language like me
and play with us at Tottingham.

ALLY McLEOD

Ach, well, delighted, y'know. For me this was a sort of
justice, y'know. In the past he had benefited from the
hand of God. This time all he got was the two fingers
of God (flicks the Vs).

OSSIE ARDILES

But to be perfectly honest, let us prefer to remember
the good things about Maradona like when he proved
to the press that he had not lost his shooting touch . . .
with an air-rifle.

ALLY McLEOD

I mean, wee Ossie's right, it's time to remember the future and that means the 1996 Eurovision Championships in England, would you believe. Anyway, the one to watch is Group 8. That's Russia, Greece, Finland, San Marino, the Faroe Islands and . . . er . . . it's another one of they diddy teams . . . oh aye, us. Of course, we didnae quite make it to America but the good news is neither did England. I hope that really pissed you off, Ray Wilkins.

RAY WILKINS

Good evening, ladies and gentlemen, mums and dads, boys and girls and a special mention to the old folks – especially all of those playing for Kilmarnock. Also hello to my old mate from my days in Italy, Liam Brady. Liam, *buongiorno amico mio, comé vai? Ti ha piacuto la coppa mondiale?*

LIAM BRADY

Er . . . *oui, beaucoup.* I've liked some of the developments, like that new ruling that in marginal offside decisions the referee should favour the attacking team 'cause I think it's about time the rest of the world was brought into line with Rangers. But it's a bit disappointing not having Scotland in the finals because we all need a laugh now and again, and I'm sure Ray Wilkins would agree.

RAY WILKINS

Absolutely . . . but I'm sure Craig Brown would disagree.

CRAIG BROWN

I thought it was a bit hard to take, the thought that all Scotland had to show at this year's World Cup was one referee. But I firmly believe if we apply ourselves properly by the time the next World Cup comes round Scotland will have *two* referees in the finals. Would you go along with that, Denis Law?

DENIS LAW

Would I go along with that? Would I . . . go along . . . with . . . that? Well, you know, as I say, the first thing we have to look at is . . . er . . . is . . . sorry, who did you say you were again?

CRAIG BROWN

Craig Brown.

DENIS LAW

Craig Brown . . . Craig Brown . . . and what is it you do, Craig?

CRAIG BROWN

I'm the manager of the Scotland *big* team.

DENIS LAW

Of course you are, of course you are, and if there's

anyone who can get Scotland back to the dizzy heights
of mediocrity it's . . . er . . . it's you . . . er . . .
Thingmae.

CRAIG BROWN

Well, in settling for mediocrity I think you're selling
Scotland short. I think we're capable of much worse
than that. But the fans will have to be patient and
allow time for my five-year plan to take effect – say
about . . . twenty years. During this time I hope to
replace passion with passing and get the players playing
not just with their hearts but using their heads – so,
obviously, Duncan Ferguson has a big part to play in
this.

DENIS LAW

Sorry, but I disagree. I happen to think that Scotland
played better when they played with heart in them.
Maybe not as good as when they played with bevvy in
them but, you know, as I say, in my day, Scotland had,
quite literally, thousands and thousands of flair players
like Baxter, Johnstone . . . Johnstone, Baxter, you
know, quite literally thousands of them, you know?

CRAIG BROWN

For me, team spirit is the most important thing and I
was very impressed with Brazil, especially the way they
held on to each other's hands as they went out to face
their opponents. Of course, this is similar to a scheme
Andy Roxburgh and I pioneered as far back as 1990 in
Italy when the Scottish players held on to each other's

hands as they climbed down the drainpipes of their hotel.

DENIS LAW

Well, you know, as I say, I was impressed by the Brazilians, especially the ones from Brazil. But, you know, as I say, Brazil 1994 are a good side, a very good side, but not a *great* side, not like the Brazilian eleven from 1970. Now would you agree with that, Ally McLeod?

ALLY McLEOD

Ach, well, tremendous, what we've got to remember, y'see, is that Brazil are Brazilians and we're not. Well, it stands to reason, so, despite all those silky skills that means they cannae qualify for the Eurovision Championships and we can, so to make sure we do, I think we should stop nitpicking at Craig Brown and just get tore right into him. Drive him to the verge of a mental flaky because it's a well-known fact that Scotland team bosses function better when they haven't a clue what they're doing.

WILLIAM McILVANNEY

The anaesthesia is wearing off. We are starting to come round from a World Cup soccerdectomy. What will be the first thing we see? The new acceptable face of our domestic game? A smiling, beckoning face, clearasil-ed of the blackheads of bureaucracy, the plooks of procrastination and the warts of waffle? For changes have been promised that will rock the game to its very foundation creams and cleanse the soccerdermus with the oil of *olé, olé, olé, olé*. As a new dawn beckons, a new chapter begins, another opportunity knocks – and I mean that most sincerely – how spectacular will our intransigence be this season? Let's go round the grounds to find out, starting at Derek Johnstone's second home – Ibrox Stadium.

DEREK JOHNSTONE

Fair dos. This is what it's all about. David Murray raises that sixth league championship flag and, of course, given Rangers' magnificent tradition, the flag is raised only halfway up the symbolic leg of the flagpole. So I take Rangers, backed by that magnificent loyal support, to win everything this year. But Davy Provan, as a traitor to your religion, I suppose you'll go for Celtic.

DAVY PROVAN

Hello Derek, yes Derek, well Derek, that is a quality assumption of quality. In the past we've all had a bit of a laugh at Celtic's expense, but I think this season Hearts could be the comedy team to watch.

DEREK JOHNSTONE

Fair dos, early doors, I hear what you're saying, Davy, as a former back four myself, I've always felt Graeme Hogg was suspect with crosses; at Starks Park he proved suspect with left hooks, too.

166

DAVY PROVAN

No doubt about it, Derek, it was a quality punch and
a slap in the face to those critics who feel Craig Levein
is a bit lightweight, injury-prone and lacks a bit of
bottle. This one act of *sheer* folly could have him back
in contention.

DEREK JOHNSTONE

As Scotland's next captain?

DAVY PROVAN

As Frank Bruno's next opponent. But all credit to the
club, popular new boss Tommy 'Hammy the Hamster'
McLean immediately called a conference and met the
press face to knee.

TOMMY McLEAN

Er . . . to be perfectly honest, I didnae see a thing . . .
er . . . what about you, John Robertson?

JOHN ROBERTSON

Not a thing, boss.

TOMMY McLEAN

But make no mistake, they'll be punished . . . at least
four of the belt and then I'll put them on the transfer
list but not sell them.

CHICK YOUNG

Ho! Ho! Ho! And still in the capital, Hibs, the Hibees,

Hibernian, the men who would be Tims, home of one of Auld Reekie's most famous landmarks, Arthur Duncan's Seat, have signed a shirt sponsorship deal with Calor Gas. Without, of course, meaning to be totally cruel, I could say, having seen Hibs in the past, that *nerve* gas would have been more appropriate. But I won't. Now if I could just bring in Derek Johnstone, I'd be crushed to death because this is a very small commentary box, but there is room for Hibs boss Alex Miller.

ALEX MILLER

Yes, hello, Chick, welcome to Easter Road, a ground where a lot of clubs can find it difficult to pick up points – especially Hibs.

CHICK YOUNG

Alex, as an ex-bluenose, it must give you the dry boak having to manage a team that plays in green. But let's move away from the injustices of life back to your current home, your ain midden, the aforementioned Easter Road with its state-of-the-art corrugated iron sheets. Alex, any plans for a new stadium?

ALEX MILLER

Definitely, but first and foremost I've got to get it right on the park and that, of course, is down to the players. At the back – well, I don't need to bandy words about, our goalkeeper, Jim Leighton, is bandy enough as it is. And upfront, well, if I can get O'Neill and Evans to fight a bit more and Darren Jackson to fight a bit *less* I think we could do something. See, Chick , I'd rather win by playing football – unfortunately, sometimes, Darren would rather win by two falls, a submission or a knockout.

CHICK YOUNG

Alex, no transfer rumours as yet so I'll start one now. I hear you've got your eye on a six-foot-four-inch Hibee who's just finished a humiliating spell down south.

ALEX MILLER

Ach no, that is an absolute lie. I have not made a move for John Leslie of *Blue Peter*.

CHICK YOUNG

And, of course, Hibs' opening game had a somewhat alien ring to it. A 5–0 phasing out of Dundee United. I'll bet you that put Golac's gas at a peep, Dick Donnelly.

DICK DONNELLY

Yes, Dick Donnelly here in a gie blawey, I may add, Festival City of Edinburgh. That's right, surprise, surprise, I've been let out of dreich, dour, dull, deadly Dundee for the day. But don't worry, I'm sure my two companions – looking very smart, I might say, in their white coats – will take good care of me. As for Auld Reekie itself, well, to be perfectly honest, I haven't seen Wallace Mercer yet, but this festival is a brilliant thing – in fact I'm off now to see a musical based on the career of former Hibs chairman, David Duff . . . It's called *Fiddler on the Roof.*

DAVY PROVAN

Hello Dick, yes Dick, well Dick, time for your medicine Dick. Davy Provan here and with me United guru Ivan Golac. Ivan, man, hardly the perfect start, a quality reaming from a team as duff as Hibs.

IVAN GOLAC

That's exa'tly what I'm just saying to players, y'know, I'll be look for big improvement for Yo-ro-pean matches but no, yes, I'm not happy man so I fine everyone two weeks' wages. That's right, one hundred pounds for bad performance. But looking on bright side of 5–0 humpering, I am very happy with consistency – we were the same level of crap for entire ninety minutes.

DAVY PROVAN

If I could just bring in Jim McLean, who's been flicking the Vs behind Ivan's back. Jim, any truth in the rumour that you pair hate each other's guts?

JIM McLEAN

No, no, no . . . on behalf of Igor, I would just like to say it is absolute rubbidge to suggest that there's any feelings, bad or otherwise, between me and *him*, and if he doesn't like that then he can get away back to Serbio.

DAVY PROVAN

So, that rift, which is like a breath of fresh air, doesn't exist and everything in the garden is rosy?

IVAN GOLAC

Exa'tly. Everything in garden is rosy . . . and tangerine and purple and psychedelic, man!

DAVY PROVAN

Ivan, quality stuff.

IVAN GOLAC

Okay, how much you got?

DAVY PROVAN

So, with the final scoreline, Hibernian five, Dundee United infinity, it's back to the studio, Ibrox Stadium.

DEREK JOHNSTONE

Well, thanks, Davy, this is what it's all about, a superb Mark Hateley header, a quite stunning Duncan Ferguson trundler both made by Man of the Match Brian Laudrup, who, after one game, must be, *must* be, Player of the Year. Judge for yourself tonight when you see it on television.

DAVY PROVAN

Now, Derek, do we know for definite the cameras were at the Rangers game?

DEREK JOHNSTONE

Well, they usually are. Now it's over, I believe, to one of the new boys.

DAVY PROVAN

That's right, and it's an old friend of yours, Derek.

TERRY BUTCHER

Hi, Terry Butcher here and what a mouth-watering match in prospect. A real menu for excitement. But if you prefer a nice meal – in convivial surroundings – then why not try the big Terry Butcher's hotel in beautiful Bridge of Allan.

CHICK YOUNG

Ho! Ho! Ho! If we could just concentrate on the football, Terry. What a character, Terry Butcher, Captain Courageous, King William Tel, leader of men, remover of doors . . .

DEREK JOHNSTONE

Woah, wait a minute. What's he doing on the show? No, I'm sorry, Chick Young, *unfair* dos. *I'm* the big jovial ex-Hun on Radio Clyde, it's as simple as that. Who else have they signed up in the close season?

DAVID SYME

Hello, yes, David Syme here at a very exciting match –

DEREK JOHNSTONE

    I don't believe it, unbelievable, David Syme? But *I'm*
the voice of Protestant reason on Clyde! What's
happening, Hugh Keevins?

HUGH KEEVINS

    In a nutshell, Derek, quite simply putting it as
succinctly as I can in a word, in a sentence, in an essay,
in a soliloquy, in a novel . . . sorry, Derek, Fergus
McCann is addressing the Celtic fans at Hampden
Park.

FERGUS McCANN *(once again, Fergus is at first facing*
    the wrong way)

    Friends, Romans, Celticmen, lend me your cash . . .
For it's a grand old team to pay for. I've been in many
exotic locations – Canada, America, Kilsyth, Croy –
but now I am come home to rebuild my beloved
Celtic.

CHICK YOUNG

    Fergus . . . time for a couple of questions?

FERGUS McCANN

    Sure, Junior, shoot.

CHICK YOUNG

    Fergus, a few months ago this club was a tic-a-tic-a-
Tim bomb waiting to explode; the Celtic faithful were
praying in their chapels, wearing down their rosary

beads and robbing their St Vincent de Paul boxes to keep their club afloat. They were facing Timageddon. Then the miracle; just as Judas and his twelve apostles raised Lazyarse from the dead, Brian and his McCanno kit reconstructed Celtic. Fergus, youse are jammy bastards.

FERGUS McCANN

Yeah, well, thanks, Chick. But as you know, in Scottish football, if you're going to get on you've got to make your own luck, or make your own lodge.

CHICK YOUNG

Great to see you're settling in, Fergus. You spoke that paranoia like a native.

FERGUS McCANN

I'm learning all the time, Chick, and I'm happy with the way things are now at Cel'ic. The rigid stubbornness has gone. We are now attractive, adaptable and flexible. We're no longer the biscuit-tin club; we are now the tupperware-box club. And I'm sure Tommy Burns will back me up on that.

CHICK YOUNG

Thomas 'Tommy' Burns, a confirmed Kilmarnock man until you were tempted by the satanic forces at Celtic Park. I hope you went to Confession after the way you gave Killie the rubber ear.

TOMMY BURNS

    Aye, well . . . eh . . . this is very very true.
Unfortunately, my move from Kilmarnock wasn't the
way I would have liked it but let's be very very honest:
tapping is something that goes on all the time. In fact,
once, when I was a player at Celtic, I was tapped by
Kevin Kelly . . . for fifty pence. I was very very
shocked but in the end I gave him it – after all, he had
watched my motor for me.

DAVY PROVAN

    Tommy, different class, as is your born-again captain,
Paul McStay. Hello, Paul, yes Paul, well Paul, how are
things with Celtic now?

PAUL McSTAY

    There's a buzz about the place, a definite buzz, you
could hear it.

DAVY PROVAN

    And do you think this has to do with Tommy Burns?

PAUL McSTAY

    No, it was to do with the electric trimmer – I was
getting a haircut.

DAVY PROVAN

    Paul, do you think this could be a new era or just
another false dawn for the club?

PAUL McSTAY

Yes, definitely, this could be a new era . . . or just another false dawn for the club, definitely, yes.

DAVY PROVAN

Paul, what about recent allegations made by someone who shall remain nameless that you, and I quote, 'couldn't shoot for toffee'?

PAUL McSTAY

Well, that's true. I couldn't shoot for toffee because I don't like toffee, it makes your fillings come out. I quite like strawberry cremes, though.

DAVY PROVAN

Paul, that is a Quality Street answer.

PAUL McSTAY

Who said that about me, anyway?

DAVY PROVAN

Dr Michael Kelly.

PAUL McSTAY

Dr *Who*?

DAVY PROVAN

Exactly. So, moving on, Paul, to the international scene . . . *(worried look on Paul's face)* . . . playing for

Scotland *(McStay, relieved, understands)*. What can you say to those critics who say you can't play in the same team as Gary McAllister?

PAUL McSTAY

I just say to those critics who say I can't play in the same team as Gary McAllister that I *can* play in the same team as Gary McAllister because, as has been said many times before . . . there's a buzz about the place.

DAVY PROVAN

Sheer quality, different class, Paul. And Derek's got a sports flash for us: Derek?

DEREK JOHNSTONE

And some late news just in. Following complaints from fans about the lack of toilet paper in the bogs at Hampden, Fergus McCann has just placed an order for ten thousand copies of *Paradise Lost* by Michael Kelly. The question is, will that now make the book a best-*smeller*?

WILLIAM McILVANNEY

League reconstruction. Stadium reconstruction. Work on Scottish football's rebuilding site is in full swing amidst the growing fear and apprehension that it is already a case of too little too late. The armchair fan is being forced away from television back to the grounds by the television programmes themselves. To understand how this could happen you only need to watch them.

JIM WHITE

Hi, Jim White here, and welcome back to *Extra Whine*, where of course the news is that we've lost Gordon McQueen so, if any of our viewers out there happens to find him, please hand him in to the nearest police station, and there's a ten-pound reward in it.

GERRY McNEE

Er . . . Jim . . . Jim . . . *(coughs)*

JIM WHITE

Sorry, Gerry, trying to say something?

GERRY McNEE

I, in fact, can exclusively reveal that the reason Gordon McQueen isn't here is because he has taken up a coaching job with Middlesbrough.

JIM WHITE

You're kidding me on, Gerry.

GERRY McNEE

No.

JIM WHITE

Stop trying to take the piss, Gerry . . . *(holds his 'earpiece', reacting as if he's receiving a message)*. Yes . . . *really?* . . . Okay . . . right . . . thanks, doll. Well apparently Gerry wasn't kidding. Big Go-Go has up

and gone-gone to Boro and the *Scotsport* camera was
there for his first session with the lads.

GORDON McQUEEN

Eh, right . . . grather lound . . . *(Bounces football; it hits
the floor and stops dead.)* Now, as youse all know,
Mildesblu . . . Mladisbro . . . Marlboro . . .
Middlesbrough is a mugnificent club and it's also a
big-name club, 'cause it's got thirteen letters in it . . .
And the manager, Bra . . . Bro . . . Bru . . . Irn Bru . . .
Bryan Robson has brunged me here for to share my
experiences with other clubs like Man . . . chu . . . Fu
man chu . . . Manchester Untied, Manchester United,
Leeds and Helen Mirren . . . Saint Helen . . . Saint
Mirren. Now this is so's we can start to win things like
shies and corners and stoat-ups and things. Because my
flootball phlilosophy . . . phlossi . . . philosophy is
simple – if they score one, then we'll score two; if they
score three, then we'll get beat. Right, you three form
yourselves into pairs and we'll start *(blows whistle)*.

JIM WHITE

God save McQueen, eh, Gerry?

GERRY McNEE

No doubt about it, Jim. *Extra Whine*'s loss is
Mliddisbloro's glain.

JIM WHITE

Sure, Gerry, right. Well, there's certainly been no
shortage of movement on the international close-

season transfer market. A cool £4.5 million saw Juventus secure the stylish services of Marseille's Didier Deschamps. Dutchman Brian Roy joined Notts Forest in a £2.5 million move. And what about Spurs? Germany's Klinsmann and Romania's Dumitrescu secured in a £4.6 million double swoop!

GERRY McNEE

And don't forget Motherwell got Stevie Woods for seventy-five thousand quid.

JIM WHITE

And, of course, Gerry, we've been doing our own bit of transfer business, haven't we, boss?

GERRY McNEE

Well, that's right. My sources tell me that I can exclusively reveal that Alan McInally will be joining us.

JIM WHITE

What made you decide to appoint Timbo . . . sorry, eh, Rambo, Gerry?

GERRY McNEE

Because I'm the Senior Sports Editor.

JIM WHITE

And a great decision it was too, Gerry. Well, let's face it, Gerry, a new season and there's a lot happening, isn't there, Gerry. For starters it's now *three* points for

a win. Do you think it will make any difference,
Gerry?

GERRY McNEE

Yes, I happen to think it will make a difference of . . .
one point.

JIM WHITE

Well spotted, Gerry. And, of course, this season we've
got two new boys, Ross County and . . . er . . .
Caledonia Thingmae. Okay, cards on the table, Gerry,
who are they?

GERRY McNEE

Well, Ross County I do know. He's a smashing young
player who could easily step up a grade and play for
the likes of Forfar, Arbroath or Aberdeen. Now
Thingmae Caledonian, on the other hand, my
sources inform me, are some mob from the Highland
League.

JIM WHITE

The Highland League! So, they're not even from
Scotland then? Well spotted, nice one, Gerry! So, to
re-cap, we've got news, views, intellectual discussion
and a lot more besides. Right, Gerry?

GERRY McNEE

Affirmative, Jim, and for racing fans, I can exclusively
guarantee that our top tipster, Jim, won't make a

Delahunt of it. And great news for armchair fans – a
new batch of furniture ads from Dougie Donnelly.

DOUGIE DONNELLY

Hello, Dougie Donnelly here, and welcome to
Sportscene, Tillicoultry, near Stirling – oh dear, sorry,
wrong channel – and coming up on tonight's
programme an in-depth profile of Dumbarton boss
Murdo McLeod where we'll be asking, where is
Dumbarton anyway? And we'll be seeing that in just a
second . . . can we? . . . no, we can't . . . yes, here it is
. . . no, it's not . . . Chick Young, any idea what else is
happening?

CHICK YOUNG

Totally no, not at all, but I do have a special good
Buddy broadcast for all my fellow Saint Mirren fans
concerned over recent events in Paris. I have been
asked by Saint Mirren Football Club to reassure all the
club's fans that although they admit there *is* a
resemblance, Jimmy Bone is definitely *not* Carlos the
Jackal. And, with that welcome reassurance in such
troubled times, it's back to you, Dougie.

DOUGIE DONNELLY

Ah, thanks, Chick, reassurance indeed and very
welcome news right now, as would be that special
report on Murdo McLeod . . . can we? . . . no, we can't
. . . well, what about the report on motocross that no
one ever watches, can we see that? Yes, we can . . .
well, coming up on tonight's programme . . . no, we

can't; no, we can't. But what I can do is tell you about our quite superb golf competition. Now as you may or may not know, in a month's time the inaugural Peter Stuveysant World Matchplay Championship, featuring *all* the top players, takes place in Hawaii and we've got two tickets to give away for a Pro-Celebrity tournament which starts on the same day in Girvan. And that's just one of the great sporting events we've got to look forward to this winter.

WILLIAM McILVANNEY

Starting, of course, with European football. Scotland's annual invasion of the continent as always inspired Churchillian passion. Never before on the field of Scottish football was so much blowed by so few for so many. Motherwell had drawn a diddy team from the Faroes and had humped them. Skonto Riga had drawn a diddy team from Scotland and had humiliated them. But a mere twenty-four hours later another result was to signal the start of a heavy period of pro-managerial tension as Rangers had their bad week. The Scottish media response was, as usual, low key.

ARCHIE MacPHERSON

Archie MacPherson here welcoming you to this special edition of *Panorama in Action* where, I put it to you, the subject for discussion is a glorious club called Rangers. Now, Chick, remind us again of just what we're talking about here.

CHICK YOUNG

Yes, Archie, total woe. In the European Cup it was *Acropolis Now*, on the Saturday it was 'Tic That, and the following Wednesday well and truly Falkirked. On top of all that you had the storming of the Basile, and all in all you're talking crisis club.

ARCHIE MacPHERSON

Oh come on, Chick – crisis club? We are talking *national disaster* here. Now, surely, and I've been saying this for years now, surely Rangers *financially* can't stand another Euro-flop. Now what I am reasonably suggesting is that the government must now raise taxes and give the extra money to Rangers.

CHICK YOUNG

It's a fair point, Archie. I'm sure the good decent subjects of Her Majesty wouldn't mind paying that bit extra if they knew it was going to a glorious cause.

ARCHIE MacPHERSON

Well, I'm not being unreasonable, am I, Davy? After all, we are the people.

DAVY PROVAN

Hello Archie, yes Archie, well Archie, no doubt about it Archie, David Murray has ploughed a fortune into Rangers Euro dream – must be the most expensive Fantasy Football game in the world. But for me, what will always hold Rangers back is a word that I know they don't like at Ibrox.

ARCHIE MacPHERSON

And that word, Davy, is 'sectarian'?

DAVY PROVAN

That word, Archie, is 'preliminary'. But Rangers are not the only business to have lost out on the dosh. Scottish Television lost a fortune in advertising revenue and I'm sure the *Extra Whine* team are bitterly disappointed because that's their Milan trip hit on the head. Of course, Gerry McNee will have his own thoughts.

GERRY McNEE

Yes, Gerry McNee here, the voice of a football, *the* Senior Sports Editor, the man who never shirks a tackle, and I can exclusively reveal that a successful European run was vital *not just* for Rangers, not just for my holiday plans but for the whole of Scotland, because if we continue with these lamentable results, Scottish clubs just won't get into the European Cup.

JIM WHITE

Too true, Gerry. That's why *everyone* in Scotland has got to support the *football* solution and get behind *every* Scottish team, especially Rangers.

GERRY McNEE

Well, absolutely correct. And I'm sure blasting 'Billy Boys' at 120 decibels out of the Ibrox PA system will do a lot to achieve this.

JIM WHITE

Too true again, Gerry. I did hear that as I was sitting in the studio on that Wednesday night, the big match itself starting after *Coronation Street*, and two things kept bugging me that night. One: is it Ay-Ee-Kay Athens or Ah-Eek Athens? And two: is Des Barnes asking for trouble with Tanya?

ARCHIE MacPHERSON

Hugh Keevins, how did you see it?

HUGH KEEVINS

Yes, it was another black, boggin', bleak, wretched, woeful, ganting, desperately awful European exit night for Rangers . . . and it pains me to say it.

ARCHIE MacPHERSON

Oh, Hugh, I put it to you that you were probably *hoping* Rangers would get beat.

HUGH KEEVINS

No, Archie, you're wrong, I was not *hoping* they'd get beat – I was on my knees *praying* they'd get beat!

ARCHIE MacPHERSON

Hugh, are you telling me that God's a Tim?

HUGH KEEVINS

Surely, Archie, you're not trying to tell me that you were ever in any doubt as to God's football allegiances?

186

He's a Celtic man through and through.

ARCHIE MacPHERSON

Well, I put it to you that Glasgow Rangers are a bit more important than God!

CHICK YOUNG

Ho! Ho! Ho'd the bus! Chick Young here sticking his neb in uninvited as usual to point out that if it wasn't for Rangers there would be no God because Walter Smith would be out of a job. But to be honest, I don't expect Radio Clyde to care about Rangers, not with those initials – and what about the BBC? It's time they started playing 'God Save the Queen' after *every* programme and rallied to the cause. After all, Donald Findlay can't do it all himself.

DONALD FINDLAY (*worried and minus scarf, talking on the phone*)

Yes, Donald Findlay here, Your Honour. Of course, Your Honour, on the level, brother, there's snow on the roof, ah yes, Your Honour, I've instructed Duncan Ferguson to take the fifth amendment and refuse to answer any questions on the grounds that he'll probably make an arse of himself. Thanks, Your Honour. Oh, Your Honour, your tickets are in the post. (*Walter Smith saunters in.*) Ah, Walter, just the man. Have you walked around the temple lately? This place is suffering one helluva hangover. It's like Larkhall on the *thirteenth* of July.

WALTER SMITH

> Well, obviously, you know, particularly, at the present moment, things are particularly bad. Some loyal burger even threw their scarf at me.

DONALD FINDLAY *(when Walter holds up the scarf, Findlay's reaction tell us it's his)*

> Really? Er . . . that's terrible . . . er . . . so, what about Monsieur Boli then, and the things he said about our tactics, our preparation, our dress code? We just can't have people wandering around telling the truth like that.

WALTER SMITH

> At the present moment I can accept criticism of tactics and obviously I will say that possibly our preparations might not have been particularly perfect. But as manager of Rangers what I will *not* have is *anyone* criticise our sleeveless cardigans. So, I warned Basile one more misdemeanour and it's the Broxy Bear costume.

DOUGIE DONNELLY

> And Dougie Donnelly here, saying you can see more of that fascinating fly-on-the-derry's-wall documentary here on BBC Scotland in tomorrow night's edition of *Foc-all Point.*

WILLIAM McILVANNEY

> Scottish football, where we love the unpredictability only when it's predictable, where we thrive on the

uncertainties only when they're certain, where we thrill to the drama of the undramatic. For if all the world's a stage then Scottish football is currently the community centre pantomime.

So how does the play conclude, what is this epic journey's end? Only time will tell if Scotland will, in the final act, rise and be that football nation again . . . or if it will disappear up its own farce.

(The lights come up, the fans are rattled, confused, trying to sort things out.)

JONNY

What's happenin'? Where am I? I can hear voices . . . confusion . . . all talkin' rubbish . . . it's like they're recording *Sport in Question* inside my head.

TONY

It's okay, I'm the same – just take it easy.

JONNY

We must've been out of it for about two hours – have we missed anything?

TONY

No. Just two eejits talkin' about football.

JONNY

See that's the problem. *Talking* about football. At least we *did* something about it.

TONY

Aye, exactly, right . . . what?

JONNY

We travelled through time . . . we had a look at the future, came back with the answers.

TONY

Sorry to disillusion you, but that was all just a dream.

JONNY

A dream? So the future is –

TONY

Just more of the past that hasn't happened yet.

JONNY

So do ye mean we're not gonna beat Albania to win the World Cup for the third time in a row?

TONY

No.

JONNY

And we're not gonna be the number-one football nation in the world?

TONY

Sorry.

JONNY

And we're not gonna beat England 7–6 in the final of the European Championship?

TONY

Oh aye, we'll do that all right.

JONNY

Nae bother.

TONY

Some people are on the pitch, they think it's all over.

JONNY

It is now.

(It's all over bar the applause. The players take their bow.)

THE END

LIFESTYLE WITH PHILIP DIFFER

Full name	Philip Differ
Previous clubs	St Billy Bremner's High, Stirling; Kilsyth Boys Club, Kilsyth; St Pat's Kilsyth Christian Crusaders; Zeala FC; Young Boys of Croy; Twechar St Germain; Ajax Queenzieburn
Present post	Senior Producer, Comedy Unit, BBC Scotland
Honours won	*Naked Radio* *A Kick Up the Eighties* *Scotch and Wry* *Naked Video* *Tackle!* *2000 Not Out* *The Ferguson Theory* *Jolly* *Pulp Video* *Only an Excuse?* (radio, television, theatre)
Previous jobs	Clerical officer, clerical assistant, clerical officer again, trainee driving instructor, mature student, writer
Mission in life	To make everyone in football pay for the fact that I never made the grade